15 Topics for Tomorrow's World

世界の未来を占う　最重要トピック 15

SHOHAKUSHA

はじめに

　人工知能の目覚しい進化、ビッグデータやそれを活用したマシンラーニングやディープラーニングといった技術革新やiPS細胞などの医療技術の発展が、予想以上の速さで産業構造や私たちの価値観や社会道徳、ひいては人間のあり方そのものを変えつつあり、今後そのスピードや程度が加速度的に増すことが予想されます。あるいは、食やプラスチック汚染や気候変動など、私たちがいま何を選択するかに近い未来の姿が大きく左右されることもあります。本書では、そのような未来を占うキーワードを通して、いま何が起きつつあり未来はどのような姿をしているのか、世界的な有力紙や最先端のニュースを扱うサイトから選んだ記事の見解をみなさんに提示します。さらに、その提示された見解に対して、みなさんがどのように反応し、どのような未来の姿を望み、どのような選択をするのか考える力を涵養してもらうのがねらいです。

　「人工知能」の進化による「高齢者介護」や「自動運転車」、「ビッグデータ活用による治安維持」や「ベーシックインカムの導入の議論」を扱う一方、若い世代の価値観の変化を窺う「画像加工した自撮りとセルフイメージ」や「LGBTや人間関係に重点を置いた新しい性教育」といった話題も取り上げています。「シェアリング経済」や「サブスクリプション経済」、「ミレニアル世代のミニマリズム志向」といったキーワードからは経済面での若い世代の価値観の変化が見て取れます。それらに通底するのは「モノの所有」から「モノの利用・体験消費」へのシフトです。主にこの点に関して、スペシャルユニットとして近頃引退した安室奈美恵さんの現象を取り上げます。通常のユニットと違って練習問題はなく、代わりに安室さんを通してどのような未来が占えるのか（占えないのか）をみなさんにディスカッションしてもらうユニットになっています。どの時点で取り上げてもらっても構いません。

宮本 文

本書の使い方

Matching Words & Phrases

これから読む本文に出てくる重要な単語やフレーズにふさわしい日本語の語義を選ぶ問題です。鍵となる語彙の意味を頭に入れておくことで、スムーズに本文を読むことができるようになります。

Reading Passages

500語以下の英語で書かれた、人工知能やビッグデータの導入による社会経済動向の変化から、食育や性教育まで、他にはない魅力的なラインナップです。重要な語句や難易度が高い語句は側注で意味が確認できるようになっています。なお、countable の名詞の場合でも a/-s は省略しています。また、確実に学習してほしい文法事項や内容のより詳しい説明などは、すぐ後の The Keys to Reading Passages で記しています。側注と The Keys to Reading Passages の助けを借り、本文の内容を把握しましょう。

Checking Your Understanding: True or False

本文の内容について書かれた英文が正しいかどうかを判断する問題です。まずテキストを一通り読み、概要が正しく把握できているのかどうかを確認しましょう。

How to Read a Paragraph

答えのヒントが書かれているパラグラフ番号を記してあります。本文中の当該パラグラフをもう一度よく読んで問題に答えましょう。

Translating into English

本文に出てきた文章の単語を並び替える英作文問題です。本文を見ずに、提示された日本語のみを参考にしながら並び替えましょう。

Listening Summary

本文の英語の要約の穴埋め問題です。本文全体の意味を大まかに掴んでいることが重要です。その上で文法や意味を考え、選択肢の中からふさわしい単語を選びましょう。また、音声を使用して答え合わせもできますから、リスニング能力の向上にも役立ちます。

Contents

Unit 1: How Artificial Intelligence Impacts Senior Care
人工知能と高齢者介護 — 1

Unit 2: China Could Be the Future of the Sharing Economy
シェアリング経済の未来は中国にあり — 7

Unit 3: Plastic Microbeads Ban Enters Force in UK
プラスチック海洋汚染へのイギリスの取り組み — 13

Unit 4: Japan Considers Crime Prediction System Using Big Data and AI
ビッグデータと人工知能を用いた犯罪予測システム — 19

Unit 5: The Toll of America's Obesity
アメリカの肥満まん延と食品業界および政府の責任 — 25

Unit 6: Sex Education Given LGBT-inclusive Overhaul in Wales
ウェールズにおけるLGBTも包括した性教育改革 — 31

Unit 7: Autonomous Cars Likely to Benefit Elderly in Future
自動運転車と高齢者の未来 — 37

Unit 8: Millennials Go Minimal
ミレニアル世代のミニマルな消費傾向 — 43

Special Unit

Namie Amuro, "The Madonna of Japan," Is Retiring, But Her Style Influence Lives on
時代とリンクし続けた安室奈美恵

49

Unit 9

Esports-FIFA's eWorld Cup Catching Up with the Real Thing
本家に迫るFIFA eワールドカップ

53

Unit 10

Is 'Snapchat Dysmorphia' Really Something to Be Worried About?
加工自撮り画像と理想の自分とのギャップ

59

Unit 11

Ending Food Ignorance: Education Is Too Important to Leave to Big Food
子供たちの食育は誰が担うのか

65

Unit 12

Tech CEOs Back Call for Basic Income as AI Job Losses Threaten Industry Backlash
IT企業のトップがベーシックインカムを支持する理由

71

Unit 13

Cramer Pinpoints the 'Best Secular Trend' in the Market: Subscription Services
「モノ所有」から「利用」へ──サブスクリプション経済のビジネスモデル

77

Unit 14

World Bank Warns Over South Asian Climate 'Hotspots' as Crops and Livelihoods Hit
気候変動と温室効果ガスに対する2つのシナリオ

83

Unit 15

First-of-its-kind Clinical Trial Will Use Reprogrammed Adult Stem Cells to Treat Parkinson's
世界初パーキンソン病へのiPS細胞治験開始

89

Acknowledgements

Unit 1: How Artificial Intelligence Impacts Senior Care
By Susan Hall. December 27, 2017 © HealthTech

Unit 2: China Could be the Future of the Sharing Economy
Must include the following copyright line in close proximity to the licensed content:
Used with permission of Bloomberg L.P. Copyright © 2017. All rights reserved.

Unit 3: Plastic microbeads ban enters force in UK
Copyright © Guardian News & Media Ltd 2018

Unit 4: Japan Considers Crime Prediction System Using Big Data and AI
From The Japan Times, June 24, 2018 © JIJI, AFP-JIJI, KYODO

Unit 5: The Toll of America's Obesity
From The New York Times, August 9 © 2018 The New York Times. All rights reserved. Used by permission and protected by the Copyright Laws of the United States. The printing, copying, redistribution, or retransmission of this Content without express written permission is prohibited.

Unit 6: Sex Education Given LGBT-inclusive Overhaul in Wales
Copyright © Guardian News & Media Ltd 2018

Unit 7: Autonomous Cars Likely to Benefit Elderly in Future
From Detroit Free Press, November 18 © 2017 Gannett-Community Publishing. All rights reserved. Used by permission and protected by the Copyright Laws of the United States. The printing, copying, redistribution, or retransmission of this Content without express written permission is prohibited.

Unit 8: Millennials Go Minimal: The Decluttering Lifestyle Trend That Is Taking Over
From Forbes.com, September 7 © 2016 Forbes. All rights reserved. Used by permission and protected by the Copyright Laws of the United States. The printing, copying, redistribution, or retransmission of this Content without express written permission is prohibited.

Special Unit: Namie Amuro, "The Madonna of Japan," Is Retiring, But Her Style Influence Lives On by Janelle Okwodu. From Vogue.com, October 21 © 2017 by Vogue.com/Janelle Okwodu. Used by permission of Janelle Okwodu. All rights reserved.

Unit 9: Esports-FIFA's eWorld Cup Catching Up With the Real Thing
From reuters.com, August 4 © 2018 reuters.com. All rights reserved. Used by permission and protected by the Copyright Laws of the United States. The printing, copying, redistribution, or retransmission of this Content without express written permission is prohibited.

Unit 10: Is 'Snapchat Dysmorphia' Really Something to be Worried about?

Unit 11: Why Isn't Nutrition Education a Priority in Public Schools?
By Michael Doherty. April 20, 2018 © One Green Planet

Unit 12: Tech CEOs Back Call for Basic Income as AI Job Losses Threaten Industry Backlash
Courtesy of CNBC

Unit 13: Cramer Pinpoints the 'Best Secular Trend' in the Market: Subscription Services
Courtesy of CNBC

Unit 14: World Bank Warns over South Asian Climate 'Hotspots' as Crops and Livelihoods Hit
© Telegraph Media Group Limited 2018

Unit 15: First-of-its-kind Clinical Trial Will Use Reprogrammed Adult Stem Cells to Treat Parkinson's
By Dennis Normile. July 30, 2018 © 2018 American Association for the Advancement of Science

Unit 1

How Artificial Intelligence Impacts Senior Care
人工知能と高齢者介護

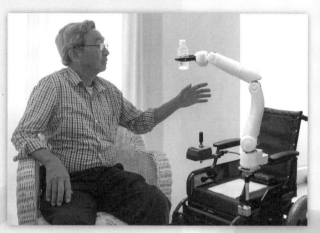

人工知能（Artificial Intelligence, AI）の活用が様々な分野で進められているなか、目覚しい成果を上げているのが医療分野である。介護者（caregiver）の不足（shortage）が予測される高齢者介護（senior care, eldercare）業界においても、人工知能は身体データを集積、パターンを認識・解析（pattern recognition and analytics）し、臨床的な意思決定支援（clinical decision support）をするところまで進んでいる。また、人との間に交友を築くコンパニオンロボット（companion robot）は、痴呆症（dementia）やアルツハイマー病（Alzheimer's disease）、うつ病（depression）の症状の進行抑制や改善に役立つことがわかってきた。

Matching Words & Phrases

1～10までの単語の語義をa～jのなかから選んで、線で結びなさい。

1. exceed
2. adoption
3. address ［動］
4. cognitive
5. what is more
6. meanwhile
7. equipped with
8. detect
9. clinician
10. expertise

a. （問題などに）取り組む
b. 検出する、発見する
c. …を装備された
d. 臨床医
e. 認知の、認知機能を高める
f. 超える
g. 専門技術、ノウハウ
h. 同時に
i. さらには、その上
j. 実行、採択

Reading Passages

[1] Artificial intelligence has made steady strides as a useful tool for healthcare professionals, and some estimate its market in the industry will exceed $5.5 billion by 2022. But what kind of promise does the technology hold for the senior care industry?

[2] Researchers continue to demonstrate AI's potential, although challenges remain for widespread adoption.

[3] A companion robot developed at the University of Denver, for example, is designed to address the projected shortage of caregivers for seniors with dementia, Alzheimer's disease and depression.

[4] The AI-programmed robot holds conversations with patients, reminds them to take their medications and leads them in light physical activity and cognitive games. Using a rear-projection design, the robot uses speech detection to respond with appropriate facial expressions to individuals.

[5] What's more, through a tablet on its chest, it can be used in reminiscence therapy by projecting family photos and stories.

[6] "I think social robotics can make a huge impact on senior care," says Mohammad H. Mahoor, associate professor in the Ritchie School of Engineering and Computer Science at the University of Denver, who leads the project.

Residents Develop a Bond with Robotics

[7] Pilots in a Denver-area senior facility have found general benefits from using the robot, Mahoor says. Researchers plan to take blood samples of individual users to determine if the robot affects biomarkers of Alzheimer's disease.

[8] Patient acceptance has not been a problem. One 86-year-old man even named the robot after his late wife, Mahoor says. "I know it sounds odd, but there's a

bond that develops," he says. "The robot has a sense of humor. It might be sassy. Sometimes it comes up with answers that make you laugh."

9 Meanwhile, research by an interdisciplinary team at the University of Missouri's Center for Eldercare and Rehabilitation Technology focuses on using sensors, pattern recognition and analytics to help seniors stay active and independent.

10 Using data from residents of TigerPlace, independent apartments equipped with sensors and RN care coordination, the center has conducted multiple projects that use both supervised and unsupervised machine learning and analytics to predict falls, detect the onset of health problems (such as urinary tract infection, low blood sugar and depression) and assess physical function.

AI Offers Senior Caregivers Decision Support

11 TigerPlace residents using the technology were able to live independently for 1.7 years longer than those without it, saving about $30,000 over the cost of a nursing home, according to the university's research.

12 "What we've done so far is basically a clinical decision support system," says Dr. Marjorie Skubic, the center's director and a professor in the engineering and computer science departments. "We rely heavily on the clinician to receive the alerts and understand what to do about them, so it does require some expertise and training."

13 The next step, Skubic says, is for AI to provide more guidance to facility staff as to what needs to be done and what might develop from particular pattern changes, bringing in more information from electronic health records to provide context.

The Keys to Reading Passages・・・・・・・・・・・・・

l. 7 …… although challenges remain for widespread adoption
(=although challenges for widespread adoption remain)「広範にわたり実行すべき数々の課題が残っているが」。

l. 15 …… rear-projection
「リアプロジェクション方式」とは、スクリーンの背面から内臓プロジェクターで映像を投影する方式。通常のプロジェクターはスクリーンの前面から映像を投影する。

l. 19 …… reminiscence therapy
「回想法」は主に高齢者を対象に行われるセラピーで、対象者が語るライフヒストリーや思い出にひたすら耳を傾けたりすることによって、回想を促す刺激を与える。認知症の予防や進行抑制、あるいは抑うつ状態の緩和などの効果が期待される。

l. 21 …… social robotics
「ソーシャルロボット工学」。ソーシャルロボットとは、人間とのコミュニケーションを主眼に置いたロボットのこと。

l. 30 …… biomarker
「バイオマーカー」とは、血中などに含まれる様々な病気の存在を示す指標のこと。

l. 44-45 …… RN care coordination
「看護師によるケア・コーディネーション（介護支援サービス管理）」。RNとは、registered nurse（正看護師）の略。

l. 46-47 …… supervised and unsupervised machine learning
「機械学習（マシンラーニング）」とは、過去の作動の蓄積から自身の動作を改良していくことのできるスーパーコンピュータの働きである。「教師あり学習」は正解付きのデータを膨大に与え、どうしてそれがそのように分類されるのか機械自らに発見させ学習させる方法。一方、「教師なし学習」は、正解のないデータを与え、データの背後にある本質的な構造を抽出させる学習法。後者は正解がない予測や分析、解析等に適しており、膨大なデータの中から機械自らに何らかのパターンなどを発見させたりするのに用いられる。

Checking Your Understanding: True or False

📝 本文の内容に照らして合っているものにはTを、間違えているものにはFを書きなさい。

1. Some calculate that the AI market in the healthcare industry will exceed more than 5 billion by 2022.

2. The companion robot cannot talk with patients with facial expressions.

3. AI enables TigerPlace residents to live by themselves longer than those without using it.

4. AI interprets the alerts and understands what to do about them.

How to Read a Paragraph

📝 以下の問いに答えなさい。なお、（　）内はヒントとなる段落番号です。

1. Paragraph 7 において、どのような研究が計画されていると述べられていますか。

   _____
   _____

2. Paragraph 8 において、マフー氏は患者がロボットを問題なく受け入れる理由をどのように説明していますか。

   _____
   _____

3. タイガープレイスでは機械学習を用いてどのようなプロジェクトがとり行われていますか。 (Paragraph 10)

   _____
   _____

Translating into English

Reading Passages を見ずに、日本語に合うように（　）内の語句を並び替えて、英文を完成させましょう。冒頭に来る語でも頭文字を小文字にしてあります。

1. コンパニオンロボットは、痴呆症やアルツハイマー病、うつ病を患う高齢者の予想される介護者不足に取り組むために考案されている。

   A (for, to, of, designed, is, address, seniors, the projected shortage, companion robot, caregivers) with dementia, Alzheimer's disease and depression.

   _____

2. 私は、ソーシャルロボット工学が高齢者介護に多大な影響を与え得ると考えている。
   (a, on, can, think, make, huge, social robotics, senior, I, care, impact)

   _____

3. 次の段階は、何がなされる必要があるかについて、人工知能が施設のスタッフにより多くのアドバイスを提供することである。

   The next step is (to, to, for, more, provide, guidance, AI, facility staff) as to (to, done, needs, be, what)

   _____

Listening Summary

CD-03

音声を聴き、□内から適切な語を選んで空欄を埋めなさい。

AI has been developing as a useful tool for clinicians and ¹(　　　) for ²(　　　). A companion robot created at the University of Denver communicates with patients with dementia, Alzheimer's disease and ³(　　　) and encourages them to do light physical activity and ⁴(　　　) games. At TigerPlace, independent apartments ⁵(　　　) with sensors and care coordination, AI ⁶(　　　) the appearance of health problems by using data from residents. Still, it is ⁷(　　　) that determine what to do about the alerts from AI at TigerPlace.

- detects
- depression
- caregivers
- clinicians
- cognitive
- equipped
- seniors

Unit 2 China Could Be the Future of the Sharing Economy
シェアリング経済の未来は中国にあり

シェアリング経済 (sharing economy) とは、インターネットを介して個人や企業が空いているモノや場所、サービス、時間などあらゆるものを、それを必要とする人たちと交換したり共有したりする経済である。その普及の背景には、インターネットやスマートフォンなどの技術革新のおかげでサービスを手軽に提供・利用しやすくなったことがあげられる。そのシェアリング経済が今、爆発的に普及しているのが中国だ。先鞭をつけたのはアメリカの企業であるが、自転車のシェアリング (bike-sharing) など中国発のシェアリングのビジネスモデルは今や東南アジアに拡大している (expand)。中国はシェアリング経済に革新 (innovation) をもたらすか。

Matching Words & Phrases

1〜10までの単語の語義を a〜j のなかから選んで、線で結びなさい。

1. launch
2. destination
3. account for...
4. optimism
5. consumption
6. skeptical
7. in effect
8. commonplace
9. transaction
10. climate

a. 懐疑的な、信用していない
b. （事業など）乗り出す、立ち上げられる
c. 取引、売買
d. 行き先（▶本文では、「投資先」の意味）
e. 事実上、実際においては
f. 雰囲気（▶「気候」の意味もある）
g. …を占める
h. 消費
i. よくあること
j. 楽観主義

Reading Passages

[1] Homegrown ride-sharing and home-sharing companies emerged in China early this decade, shortly after Uber Inc. and Airbnb Inc. launched in the United States. The industry has boomed ever since. According to the Chinese government's sharing-economy research office, 600 million Chinese conducted business worth $500 billion in the sector in 2016, up 103 percent over 2015.

[2] Numbers like that attract investors: Chinese sharing companies raised almost $25 billion last year. The sector has grown well beyond cars and apartments: Bike sharing has been one of the country's most visible destinations for venture capital over the last few months. Even as much of the Chinese economy is slowing or stalling, the government expects China's sharing economy to account for 10 percent of GDP by 2020.

[3] Three factors justify that optimism. The first is China's demographic profile. At one end of the spectrum, China's millennials are the engine for the country's world-beating e-commerce industry and the sharing economy that's grown out of it. Rather than splurge on a car many Chinese youth would prefer to save money for lifestyle experiences such as travel, or to seed their own startups.

[4] The second factor is the rapidly changing nature of Chinese consumption. Skeptical about product safety, faced with rising home prices and burdened by the responsibility of caring for those aging parents, middle-class Chinese report they're becoming more discriminating in how they spend their money. That's propelling a well-documented shift away from mass-market products toward premium products and services. This has a twofold effect. First, money that might have been spent on, say, a car, is instead saved by ride-sharing and applied to other, premium purchases. Second, sharing enables access to premium experiences

— say, via a very good home share during a vacation. Interestingly, this trend parallels the growth of a rich, e-commerce based trade in secondhand goods (in effect, long-term sharing businesses), including luxury items like Gucci handbags.

5 The third and most important factor is the Chinese consumer's embrace of mobile payment systems. Chinese mobile-based payments were 50 times greater than those in the U.S. in 2016. These days, it's commonplace to see Chinese consumers waving their phones in front of a payment terminal, or scanning a QR code to complete a transaction which, in many cases, might be for a very small sum. (A typical Chinese bike-share requires payments that range from $0.07 to $0.14 per 30-minute ride.)

6 This welcoming climate means many of the world's innovations in sharing businesses may start coming out of China, rather than Silicon Valley. Already Chinese bike-sharing companies are expanding into and being copied in Southeast Asia, spreading a business model built for China's peculiar transportation challenges. And soon China's vast manufacturing base may give rise to an app-based sharing economy of its own, providing small manufacturers access to 3D printers and other equipment. Sure, there will be boondoggles and busts along the way. But one day, China may be the one teaching the world how to share.

The Keys to Reading Passages

l. 2-3 …… Uber Inc.
「ウーバーテクノロジー社」は、同名（Uber）の自動車配車ウェブサイト及び配車アプリを提供する会社。下記のAirbnbと同様、プラットフォーム（提供者と利用者をつなぐビジネスの場）を提供する業態で事業を行なっている。2009年設立。

l. 3 …… Airbnb Inc.
「エアービーアンドビー株式会社」は、民泊のプラットフォームを提供する企業。2008年設立。

l. 12 …… venture capital
「ベンチャーキャピタル」とは、ベンチャー企業に投資する会社や資本のこと。

l. 18 …… millennials
「ミレニアル世代」は、元々はアメリカで1981-1996生まれの2000年代に成年期を迎えた世代を指す。ここでは中国におけるミレニアル世代について言及されている。ミレニアル世代についてUnit 8でも詳細に扱う。

l. 42 …… mobile(-based) payment
「モバイル決済」とは、スマートフォンなどのモバイル端末を使って行なう電子決済サービスの総称。

l. 46 …… QR code
「QRコード」とは、二次元バーコードの一種で、携帯電話やスマートフォンによるURLの読み取りなどに使われる。従来のバーコードより情報量が多い。

Checking Your Understanding: True or False

本文の内容に照らして合っているものにはTを、間違えているものにはFを書きなさい。

1. The transaction amount in China's sharing economy in 2016 more than doubled over 2015.

2. Venture capital's investment in China's sharing economy has been decreasing.

3. Middle-class Chinese are skeptical about product safety and faced with dropping home prices.

4. 3D printers would be available for small manufacturers in sharing economy.

How to Read a Paragraph

以下の問いに答えなさい。なお、（ ）内はヒントとなる段落番号です。

1. ミレニアル世代が中国のシェアリング経済隆盛の原動力になっているのは、彼らのどのような傾向によるところが大きいですか。(Paragraph 3)

2. 中国の消費の性質はどのように変化していますか。(Paragraph 4)

3. 中国のモバイル決済の特徴を挙げなさい。(Paragraph 5)

Translating into English

📝 Reading Passages を見ずに、日本語に合うように（　）内の語句を並べ替えて、英文を完成させましょう。冒頭に来る語でも頭文字を小文字にしてあります。

1. 自転車のシェアリングは、過去数ヶ月の間、その国の最も目立ったベンチャーキャピタルの投資先の一つになっている。

   (the, of, for, been, has, visible, country's, most, one, bike sharing, venture capital, destinations) over the last few months.

   _____

2. 自動車に使われてきたかもしれないお金は、ライドシェアによって貯金される。

   Money (a, on, by, is, might, have, spent, saved, been, that, car, ride-sharing).

   _____

3. 2016年において、中国のモバイル決済はアメリカのそれよりも50倍多かった。

   (were, than, in the U.S., mobile-based, greater, those, times, payments, Chinese, 50) in 2016.

   _____

Listening Summary

CD-05

📝 音声を聴き、☐内から適切な語を選んで空欄を埋めなさい。

> There are three reasons why China's sharing economy has been growing rapidly. First, China's ¹(　　　) would prefer to save money for lifestyle experiences rather than waste money on a car. Second, the nature of Chinese ²(　　　) has been shifting from ³(　　　) products toward ⁴(　　　) products and services. Sharing businesses ⁵(　　　) access to premium experiences and luxury items. Finally, ⁶(　　　) payment systems have been spreading among Chinese ⁷(　　　). Soon China will be the leading country in sharing economies in the world.

- consumption
- mobile-based
- premium
- mass-market
- consumers
- enable
- millennials

Unit 3

Plastic Microbeads Ban Enters Force in UK

プラスチック海洋汚染へのイギリスの取り組み

日本ではマイクロプラスチックと呼ばれることが一般的なマイクロプラスチックビーズ (plastic microbead) は、5mm 以下の微細なプラスチックの破片 (debris) のごみ (litter) を指す。最近になり、これが海洋において深刻なプラスチック汚染 (plastic pollution) を引き起こしていることがわかり、各国が規制や対策に乗り出した。イギリスでは 2018 年 1 月より、マイクロプラスチックビーズを含んだ角質除去用 (exfoliating) のフェイススクラブ (face scrub) や歯磨き粉 (tooth paste) といったパーソナルケア用品 (personal care product) の製造が禁止となった。しかし、ペットボトル (plastic bottles) などの使い捨て (single-use) プラスチック容器への対策など、取り組むべき問題は山積している。

Matching Words & Phrases

1〜10 までの単語の語義を a〜j のなかから選んで、線で結びなさい。

1. ban
2. pledge
3. asset
4. tackle
5. devastate
6. charge
7. make a difference
8. sentence
9. convict
10. abuse

a. 取り組む
b. 効果がある
c. 有罪と宣告する
d. 資産
e. 誓う
f. 荒らす
g. 課徴金
h. 禁止（する）
i. 虐待（する）
j. 判決

Reading Passages

1 Plastic microbeads can no longer be used in cosmetics and personal care products in the UK, after a long-promised ban came into effect on Tuesday. The ban initially bars the manufacture of such products and a ban on sales will follow in July.

2 Thousands of tonnes of plastic microbeads from products such as exfoliating face scrubs and toothpastes wash into the sea every year, where they harm wildlife and can ultimately be eaten by people. The UK government first pledged to ban plastic microbeads in September 2016, following a US ban in 2015.

3 The huge problem of plastic pollution choking the oceans has gained a high profile with recent revelations that there are five trillion pieces of plastic floating in the world's seas and that the debris has reached the most remote parts of the oceans. Microbeads are a small but significant part of this which campaigners argued was the easiest to prevent.

4 "The world's oceans are some of our most valuable natural assets and I am determined we act now to tackle the plastic that devastates our precious marine life," said environment minister Thérèse Coffey. "Now we have reached this important milestone, we will explore how we can build on our world-leading ban and tackle other forms of plastic waste."

5 Dilyana Mihaylova, at Fauna & Flora International, said: "We are delighted that a robust UK microbeads ban comes into force today. We hope this ban signals the dawn of a new era in the fight for cleaner, healthier oceans."

6 Pressure is now mounting for action on plastic bottles – a million are bought every minute around the world and they make up a third of the plastic litter in the seas. In December, the UK's environmental audit committee (EAC) of MPs called for a deposit return scheme, which

has successfully increased recycling rates in other countries.

[7] Mary Creagh MP, EAC chair, said: "The microbead ban is a step in the right direction, but much more needs to be done. Since we called for a ban, my committee has also recommended the deposit return scheme, a latte levy for plastic-lined coffee cups and reforms to make producers responsible for their packaging. We look forward to hearing the government's response."

[8] On Sunday, the prime minister, Theresa May tweeted: "In 2015 we introduced the 5p charge on plastic carrier bags, we now see 9bn fewer bags being used. It's making a real difference. We want to do the same with single-use plastics. Nobody who watched #BluePlanet2 will doubt the need for us to do something — and we will."

[9] May's government has signalled a series of environmental moves, including a ban on ivory sales and on wild animals in circuses, as well as tougher sentences for those convicted of abusing animals and retracting a manifesto pledge on a parliamentary vote to reinstate fox hunting.

The Keys to Reading Passages

l. 6 …… tonne
1メートルトン（metric ton）= 1000kg。それに対して、ton はイギリスにおいては 1 ton ≒ 1016.1kg、アメリカにおいては 1 ton ≒ 907.2kg である。

l. 26 …… Fauna & Flora International
「ファウナ＆フローラインターナショナル」は、1903年、世界で初めて設立された自然保護団体。fauna（動物相）と flora（植物相）も合わせて覚えておこう。

l. 28 …… come into force
この Unit のタイトルの enter (into) force も同様の意味。l. 3 の come into effect も同じ。

l. 35 …… deposit return scheme
deposit は「預かり金」で、scheme は「政策、構想」。ペットボトル購入時にデポジットを払い、空のボトルを返却した時に返金が受けられる。

l. 41-42 …… latte levy
「ラテ課徴金」とは、使い捨てコーヒーカップ1個につき25ペンスを課す案。イギリスでは毎年、25億もの使い捨てコーヒーカップが使用されており、3万トンのゴミとなっている。

l. 42 …… plastic-lined coffee cup
「プラスチックが裏側に貼られたコーヒーカップ」。line は「（内側を）裏打ちする、補強する」、liner は「裏地、裏張り」の意味がある。使い捨てコーヒーカップは、紙の内側にポリエチレンが貼られており、リサイクルが極めて難しく、リサイクル率はたったの0.25％である。

l. 42-43 …… reforms...packaging
「製造した梱包容器に対して製造者に責任を負わせるための改革」。具体的には、リサイクル材料の使用を促進したり、リサイクルに適したものを製造した場合には報奨金を出したり、リサイクルやリユースが難しい梱包容器にはコストを課したりするといったもの。

l. 49 …… #BluePlanet2
"Blue Planet II" はイギリス BBC 制作の海洋ドキュメンタリーで、#BluePlanet2 はツイッターなどの SNS のハッシュタグ（検索機能）である。

l. 54-56 …… reacting...fox hunting
「キツネ狩りの復活を議会投票にかけるという公約の撤回」。キツネ狩りは伝統的な上流階級の遊びとして続けられてきたが、多くの批判から2005年に労働党政権のもとで禁止する法案が可決された（当時、メイ首相は禁止反対に投票）。保守党政権下で、キツネ狩り禁止の法案の廃止を求めた動きがあり、禁止見直しを議会投票にかけることを保守党の公約に含めるとメイ首相が公言する場面もあった。しかし、本文の通り、2018年になるとメイ首相はこの公約自体、撤回した。

Checking Your Understanding: True or False

本文の内容に照らして合っているものには T を、間違えているものには F を書きなさい。

1. Cosmetics and personal care products with microbeads can no longer be sold after January 2018 in the UK. ☐

2. The UK is the first country to ban plastic microbeads. ☐

3. The deposit return scheme makes a difference in some countries. ☐

4. May's government adds tougher sentences for convicted animal abusers. ☐

How to Read a Paragraph

以下の問いに答えなさい。なお、（ ）内はヒントとなる段落番号です。

1. パーソナルケア商品に含まれるマイクロプラスチックビーズは使用されたあと、どのような過程をたどりますか。(Paragraph 2)

2. EAC はマイクロプラスチックビーズ対策として次にどのような手を考えていますか。3 つ挙げなさい。(Paragraph 7)

3. プラスチック問題に関して、2015 年イギリスではどのような対策が導入され、どのような成果をあげていますか。(Paragraph 8)

Translating into English

Reading Passages を見ずに、日本語に合うように（　　）内の語句を並び替えて、英文を完成させましょう。冒頭に来る語でも頭文字を小文字にしてあります。

1. マイクロビーズは、このことのわずかではあるが重要な部分を担っており、活動家が議論するには、最も容易に防げる部分である。

   Microbeads are (a, part, significant, small, this, of, but) which (was, to, argued, prevent, the, easiest, campaigners).

   _____

2. 我々が我々の貴重な海洋生物を荒らすプラスチックに取り組むために行動を起こすことを私は決意している。

   I am determined we (to, the, that, our, precious, act, tackle, devastates, marine life, plastic).

   _____

3. ペットボトルは海のプラスチックごみの三分の一を占める。

   (a, the, of, up, third, make, plastic litter, plastic bottles) in the seas.

   _____

Listening Summary

CD-07

音声を聴き、□内から適切な語を選んで空欄を埋めなさい。

Plastic ¹(　　　　) is one of the greatest threats to ocean health worldwide. There are five ²(　　　　) pieces of plastic floating in the world's oceans which ³(　　　　) marine life. The UK government ⁴(　　　　) to ban plastic microbeads in 2016 and a ban on the manufacture of products containing microbeads came into ⁵(　　　　) in January 2018. The next step is to ⁶(　　　　) plastic bottles and other ⁷(　　　　) plastics.

- force ● single-use ● pollution ● pledged ● tackle ● devastate ● trillion

Unit 4

Japan Considers Crime Prediction System Using Big Data and AI
ビッグデータと人工知能を用いた犯罪予測システム

人工知能（AI）とビッグデータ (big data) を用いて街頭犯罪 (street crime) を未然に防ぐ犯罪予測システム (crime prediction system) の導入を、日本も検討しはじめた。発生場所や時刻やその他、あらゆる要因をビッグデータに取り込み、犯罪発生率が高そうな地域を割り出し、事前に対策を講じるのだ。欧米では既に一定の成果をあげている。しかしながら、人権侵害など懸念の声もあがっている。例えば、中国では顔を始め、あらゆる個人データを収集したビッグデータを用いて、個人の行動を監視する (surveil) 高度なシステムを反体制的な (restive) 地域で配備している (deploy)。犯罪予測システムは恩恵なのか、それとも監視社会の入り口なのだろうか。

Matching Words & Phrases

1〜10までの単語の語義をa〜jのなかから選んで、線で結びなさい。

1. eventually
2. fall prey to
3. vulnerable to
4. realm
5. scrutinize
6. incorporate
7. prefecture
8. employ
9. encompass
10. statistics

a. （被害に）遭いやすい（▶「弱い」が大元の意味）
b. 精査する
c. 用いる
d. 県（▶都道府県の単位）
e. 結局、ついには
f. 統計学
g. 領域、範囲
h. 網羅する
i. 犠牲になる
j. 組み込む

Reading Passages

[1] The government and the police are discussing the idea of developing a computer system that can predict street crime by utilizing big data and artificial intelligence. They hope such a system will be able to show them where and how to take greater measures to prevent crime.

[2] Street crime prediction "has already achieved results in Europe and the United States," said Mami Kajita, who established the data-analysis company Singular Perturbations Inc. last year in hopes of developing a Japanese version of the methods used in the United States. In some parts of America, the police have ramped up patrols in areas where AI-based systems predicted crime was more likely to happen, achieving a reduction of 20 percent on average, Kajita said.

[3] A more cautionary tale comes from China, where the government is racing ahead to use big data and facial recognition technology to surveil the population. According to Human Rights Watch, an advanced system called the Integrated Joint Operations Platform is pooling data on people from many sources. It has already been deployed in the restive western Xinjiang region, where it is being used to flag and detain people deemed potential threats.

[4] Kajita, 35, who studied theoretical physics at the University of Tokyo, once lived in Italy. Her husband, also a researcher, was eventually transferred there as well. They often fell prey to pickpockets. She realized that people are vulnerable to crime when they are not familiar with their surroundings. She then came up with the idea of applying her mathematical research on natural phenomena to the realm of urban phenomena to prevent crime.

[5] Kajita scrutinized the Tokyo Metropolitan Police Department's email regarding cases of molestation, theft

and suspicious people. Combining the data with her own original algorithm, Kajita predicted which areas were likely to see high levels of crime.

6 Despite her limited data, the predictions mostly matched areas where crimes actually occurred. Her accuracy is likely to improve if additional factors such as weather, traffic and Twitter posts are incorporated. "We need to continue examining crime mechanisms unique to Japan," Kajita said. "I hope to create a smartphone app for citizens in order to reduce the number of crimes, even if only slightly," Kajita said.

7 Kanagawa in January announced plans to become the first prefecture in the nation to introduce predictive policing, and hopes to put such a system in place on a trial basis before the 2020 Tokyo Olympics.

8 The AI-based system would employ a "deep learning" algorithm that allows the computer to teach itself by analyzing big data. It would encompass the fields of criminology, mathematics and statistics while gathering data on times, places, weather and geographical conditions as well as other aspects of crimes and accidents.

The Keys to Reading Passages

l. 3 …… big data
「ビッグデータ」とは、人間の行動などによって生み出され、その行動パターンや傾向などをコンピュータで分析するために使われる極めて膨大なデータ。

l. 18 …… facial recognition technology
「顔認識技術」とは、顔画像のビッグデータから導き出された、人物を自動的に識別する技術であり、本人確認に使用されたり、監視カメラのデジタル画像から個人を特定するなど多岐にわたり使用が広がりつつある。それゆえに人権的に問題があるとの懸念も大きい。

l. 19 …… Human Rights Watch
「ヒューマン・ライツ・ウォッチ」は非営利の国際人権組織。

l. 20 …… the Integrated Joint Operations Platform
「統合集積操作プラットフォーム」とは、「監視カメラ映像や身分証カードのチェック、電話やコンピュータでのWiFi接続、カルテ、銀行取引記録、法定記録を集積処理したビッグデータを使った監視システム」。(HP「地球最期のニュースと資料 In Deep」より)

l. 22 …… Xinjiang
中国の西端に位置する新疆（しんきょう）（新疆ウイグル自治区）は、ウイグル族の他に様々な民族が居住する多民族地域で、民族自治拡大を求める動きや中央からの分離独立の動きがあるため、中国当局による人権弾圧が強く、本文にもある通り、中国全土に先立ち、顔や彩虹（目）など様々な生体認証が導入され著しい監視社会となっている。

l. 37 …… algorithm
「アルゴリズム」とは、コンピュータが効率的に問題を解いたり、課題を解決したりするための処理手順。プログラミング言語で「アルゴリズム」を記述したものがコンピュータ・プログラムである。

l. 44 …… app
「アプリ」とは、application（アプリケーション）の略で、OS上で動くソフトウェアのこと。例えば、ゲームやメール、ワードなどもアプリの一種である。

l. 48-49 …… predictive policing
「予測警備」とは、犯罪の可能性を予測し、未然に防ぐ体制のこと。

l. 51 …… deep learning
「深層学習」とは、機械学習の一種であり、それをさらに進化させたもの。人間の神経を模したニューラル・ネットワークを使い、大量のデータの持つ特徴量（目の付けどころ）を人間の指示なしに自動的に学習・抽出していく。また機械学習が入力データと出力データ（特徴量）との間に明確なルールがあるのに対して、深層学習ではどうしてそのような結論に至ったのかはブラックボックスである点が大きく違う。

Checking Your Understanding: True or False

📝 本文の内容に照らして合っているものにはTを、間違えているものにはFを書きなさい。

1. Japan hesitates to employ street crime prediction.　☐

2. The United States deploys the system using facial recognition to surveil people.　☐

3. Kajita made almost correct predictions about areas where crimes were more likely to happen.　☐

4. Kanagawa plans to run a trial on predictive policing.　☐

How to Read a Paragraph

📝 以下の問いに答えなさい。なお、（ ）内はヒントとなる段落番号です。

1. アメリカでは、街頭犯罪予測システムを使ってどのようなことが実施され、どのような成果が得られましたか。(Paragraph 2)

   _____

   _____

2. ヒューマン・ライツ・ウォッチによれば、中国政府は "the Integrated Joint Operations Platform" (l. 20) を新疆に配備することによって、どのようなことを行なっていますか。(Paragraph 3)

   _____

   _____

3. どのようなことをすれば、梶田氏のシステムの精度は上がりそうですか。(Paragraph 6)

   _____

   _____

Unit 4

Translating into English

Reading Passages を見ずに、日本語に合うように（　）内の語句を並び替えて、英文を完成させましょう。冒頭に来る語でも頭文字を小文字にしてあります。

1. 彼女は犯罪を防止するために自分の自然現象に関する数学的研究を都市での現象の領域に適用するという考えを思いついた。

   She (the, on, of, with, up, her, applying, came, idea, mathematical research, natural phenomena) to the realm of urban phenomena to prevent crime.

2. 我々は日本特有の犯罪メカニズムを検証し続ける必要がある。

   (to, to, unique, continue, need, examining, we, crime mechanisms) Japan.

3. 人工知能ベースのそのシステムはビッグデータを分析することによってコンピュータが独学できるようになる「深層学習」アルゴリズムを用いることになるだろう。

   The AI-based system would employ (a, the, to, teach, allows, that, computer, itself, "deep learning" algorithm) by analyzing big data.

Listening Summary

CD-09

音声を聴き、☐内から適切な語を選んで空欄を埋めなさい。

Japan is considering developing a computer system that can ¹(　　　　) street crime by utilizing big data and AI. Kanagawa ²(　　　　) has decided to introduce predictive policing with an AI-based system which ³(　　　　) a "deep learning" ⁴(　　　　). Such a system has already been achieved in Europe and the United States. However, Human Rights Watch Organization is concerned about the fact that the Chinese government has ⁵(　　　　) a system using big data and facial recognition in Xinjiang to ⁶(　　　　) and detain people who are regarded as ⁷(　　　　) threats.

- predict
- potential
- employs
- flag
- prefecture
- algorithm
- deployed

Unit 5 The Toll of America's Obesity
アメリカの肥満まん延と食品業界および政府の責任

肥満のまん延 (the obesity epidemic) は世界的な問題となりつつあるが、とりわけアメリカでは深刻である。2015年から2016年のデータによると、アメリカ人の成人の40％近くが肥満であり、その割合は年々高くなっていっている。アメリカの肥満のまん延はもはや個人の体を蝕むだけでなく、膨大な損害 (toll) を国にもたらしている。ここで大きな問いが浮かぶ。果たして、肥満は個人の責任なのだろうか、また個人で解決できる問題なのだろうか。筆者の答えはノーであり、国家レベルでの取り組みを提言する。その提言から見えてくるのは、アメリカの食品業界とその食環境への影響力の大きさである。いま何を食べるかが人と未来を作るのだ。

Matching Words & Phrases

1〜10までの単語の語義をa〜jのなかから選んで、線で結びなさい。

1. obesity
2. contribute to...
3. diet
4. expenditure
5. commodity
6. fragment
7. manipulative
8. conventional
9. nutrition
10. epidemic

a. 支出
b. 寸断する、バラバラにする
c. 食事、食生活
d. 栄養
e. まん延（▶「伝染病」の意味もあり）
f. 従来型の、慣習的な
g. 思い通りに操るのが巧い、巧みに操作する
h. 肥満
i. 商品、産物
j. …の原因となる

Reading Passages

[1] This burden on our bodies — as well as the effects of poor diet and inadequate physical activity at any weight — contributed to declines in life expectancy in 2015 and 2016.

[2] Beyond the toll of human suffering, obesity and diet-related diseases impose massive and rapidly growing economic costs.

[3] According to the American Diabetes Association, the annual cost of diabetes in 2017 was $327 billion, including $237 billion in direct medical expenditures and $90 billion in reduced worker productivity. (More than 90 percent of diabetes cases are Type 2, which is strongly associated with obesity.) The total impact of obesity and its related complications on the United States' economic output has been estimated at between 4 and 8 percent of gross domestic product. Even on the lower end, that's comparable to the 2018 defense budget ($643 billion) and Medicare ($588 billion).

[4] Seventy percent of American adults are at least overweight, and body weight is strongly influenced by biology; we can't blame individuals and expect personal responsibility to solve the problem. Instead, we need the government to pass a suite of policy changes to encourage healthy diets.

[5] Right now the government is doing the opposite. Farm policies have made low-nutritional commodities exceptionally cheap, providing the food industry with enormous incentive to market processed foods comprised mainly of refined grains and added sugars. In contrast, vegetables, whole fruits, legumes, nuts and high-quality proteins are much more expensive. And as cheap calories have flooded the environment, opportunities to burn off those calories at school, in recreation and through physically active modes of transportation have declined.

[6] Here are some steps that could move us from a

disease-producing dietary environment to a health-promoting one:

⑦ First, establish a federal commission to coordinate obesity policy, which is now fragmented among numerous federal, state and local agencies. This commission would serve as a counterweight to the corrosive political influence and manipulative marketing practices of "Big Food" manufacturers.

⑧ Second, adequately fund obesity research into innovative approaches for prevention and treatment, beyond the conventional focus on eating less and moving more.

⑨ Third, impose a tax on processed foods, and use the proceeds to subsidize whole foods.

⑩ Fourth, prioritize the quality of the nutrition in the National School Lunch Program and Supplemental Nutrition Assistance Program. Despite some recent improvements in school lunches, too often, cafeterias still look like fast food courts. It wouldn't cost that much to invest in kitchens and train cafeteria workers so that schools could produce tasty meals from scratch with fresh vegetables and fruits, beans, minimally processed grains and healthful proteins.

⑪ Fifth, ban junk food advertising to young children, as recommended by the American Academy of Pediatrics and practiced in some European countries. Research shows that children below the age of 8 years are cognitively and psychologically defenseless against the manipulation of advertisements.

⑫ These policies would help us reverse the obesity epidemic, improve the health and financial well-being of millions, decrease inequality, halt the decline in life expectancy.

The Keys to Reading Passages

l. 20⋯⋯ overweight

WHO（世界保健機関）のHPによれば、overweight（太り過ぎ）はBMI25以上、obesity（肥満）はBMI30以上と定義されている。

l. 42-43⋯⋯ "Big Food"

アメリカの食品製造業界は大手食品会社の寡占(かせん)状態であり、大手トップ10の企業が全米の半分以上の食品を販売しているという驚くべき状況である。それらが生産・製造・販売する食品を「ビッグフード」と呼ぶ。「ビッグフード」の商品はかなり加工された食品であり、大量の砂糖、精製された炭水化物、脂肪、塩、添加物などがたっぷりと入っており、栄養価の面でも問題視されている。また肥満のまん延やそれに伴う病気との関連性も指摘されている。

l. 49⋯⋯ whole food

「自然食品」。手を加えていない野菜や果物を指すことが多い。l. 30のwhole fruitsも同様。反意語はl. 28のprocessed food。

l. 50-51⋯⋯ the National School Lunch Program

「全米学校給食プログラム」(NSLP)は1964年から始まった制度で、公立校を始めとした様々な学校で実施されており、昼食を（場合によっては朝食も）給食として提供するプログラムである。但し、給食を利用するかは個人の選択による。プログラムは農務省から補助を受け、家庭の所得に応じて無料、減額、全額の費用負担に分かれ、低所得家庭の子供がきちんとした食事を取れるようになっている。オバマ政権時代、元大統領夫人ミシェル・オバマは子供の肥満撲滅キャンペーンLet's Moveを立ち上げ、栄養基準の規制を強め、果物や野菜を使った健康的な学校給食の提供を促進する法律（Healthy Hunger-Free Kids Act、通称「ヘルシー法」）の制定（2010年）に尽力した。その結果、農務省の補助金も大幅に増えた。しかしながら、トランプ政権になりNSLPの栄養基準の規制は緩和され、農務省の予算も大幅にカットされた。

l. 51-52⋯⋯ (the) Supplemental Nutrition Assistance Program

「補助的栄養支援プログラム」(SNAP)、別名「フードスタンプ」(Food Stamp)でよく知られている、アメリカにおいて低所得者向けに実施されている公的扶助の一種で、金券の一種であるバウチャー（voucher）が支給され、スーパーマーケットで食料品を購入することができる。

Checking Your Understanding: True or False

📝 本文の内容に照らして合っているものにはTを、間違えているものにはFを書きなさい。

1. Obesity caused declines in life expectancy in 2015 and 2016. ☐

2. Individuals are responsible for obesity and overweight. ☐

3. Cheap calories have been easily available, while children have had more opportunities to burn off those calories at school. ☐

4. "Big Food" manufacturers sell products in a manipulative manner. ☐

How to Read a Paragraph

📝 以下の問いに答えなさい。なお、（ ）内はヒントとなる段落番号です。

1. 肥満および肥満に関わる複雑な要因がアメリカの経済産出量に与える影響はどのくらいですか。
   (Paragraph 3)

   _____
   _____

2. アメリカの農業政策の結果、どのようなものが安くなりどのようなものが高くなっていますか。
   (Paragraph 5)

   _____
   _____

3. 筆者はなぜ小さな子供に対するジャンクフードの広告禁止を訴えているのですか。
   (Paragraph 11)

   _____
   _____

Translating into English

Reading Passages を見ずに、日本語に合うように（　）内の語句を並び替えて、英文を完成させましょう。冒頭に来る語でも頭文字を小文字にしてあります。

1. 人が苦しむという損害以上に、肥満と食事関連の病気は、膨大な急速に増加する経済的コストを負わせる。

   Beyond the toll of human suffering, (and, and, massive, economic, rapidly, impose, growing, obesity, costs, diet-related diseases).

   _____

2. 病気を生み出す食糧環境から健康を促進する環境に私たちを進ませることができるいくつかのステップを列挙する。

   Here are (a, a, that, to, from, could, some, move, dietary environment, steps, health-promoting, disease-producing, us) one.

   _____

3. 最近の学校給食におけるいくつかの改善にも関わらず、学食がなおもファストフード・コートのように見えることがあまりにも頻繁にある。

   (in, some, despite, recent, school, improvements, lunches), too often, (like, still, look, cafeterias, fast food courts).

   _____

Listening Summary

CD-11

音声を聴き、□内から適切な語を選んで空欄を埋めなさい。冒頭に来る語でも頭文字を小文字にしてあります。

¹(　　　　) and diet-related diseases not only damage the health and financial ²(　　　　) of individuals, but also impose a great burden on the United States' economic ³(　　　　), which is comparable to the defense ⁴(　　　　) and Medicare in 2018. Only the government can solve the problem by passing a suite of policy changes to promote healthy ⁵(　　　　). For example, the government should impose a tax on ⁶(　　　　) foods and use the revenue to support ⁷(　　　　) foods.

- obesity
- whole
- diets
- processed
- budget
- well-being
- output

Unit 6 Sex Education Given LGBT-inclusive Overhaul in Wales

ウェールズにおけるLGBTも包括した性教育改革

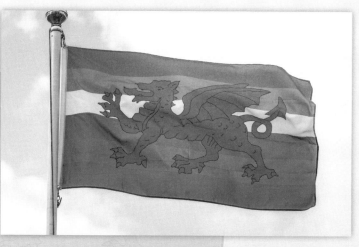

ウェールズ（Wales）も含めたイギリスでは2017年3月にそれまでの性教育のカリキュラムを改革することが発表され、2022年の実施を目指し大幅に改定されることになった。「人間関係と性の教育」(Relationships and Sex Education, RSE) と名称も変わることになった性教育はLGBT（性的マイノリティ）に関することも包括されることになり、必修科目として初めてどの教室でもLGBTの子供たちが当事者として扱われることになる。また、科目名に「人間関係」が入っていることからわかるように、性教育が単に生物学的 (biological) な話にとどまらず、家族内や社会における人と人との健全な関係性のあり方・築き方を学ぶことができ、自尊心を育むようなカリキュラムになることが期待されている。

Matching Words & Phrases

1〜10までの単語の語義をa〜jのなかから選んで、線で結びなさい。

1. given ［前］
2. overhaul
3. domestic abuse
4. diversity
5. embed
6. lobby ［動］
7. legacy
8. unreliable
9. identify
10. eradicate

a. 家庭内暴力
b. ロビー活動をする、陳述を行なう
c. 全面的な見直し
d. 根絶する
e. 明らかにする、突き止める
f. 組み込む
g. 多様性
h. 「考慮する」（▶ 接続詞的用法として「…を考慮すると、…とすれば」の意味もあり）
i. 遺物、遺産
j. 信頼を欠く

Reading Passages

[1] Wales could soon be "leading the way" in relationships and sex education (RSE) in schools after announcing an overhaul of its curriculum.

[2] The changes, which include the subject being renamed relationships and sexuality education, were announced by Wales's education secretary, Kirsty Williams, who said the days of traditional sex education were "long gone".

[3] In a departure from the traditional teaching approaches, and coming 30 years after the introduction of section 28, which banned the "promotion of homosexuality in schools", the subject will be LGBT inclusive. It will also focus on wider issues such as consent, domestic abuse and respecting diversity.

[4] It will form a statutory part of Wales's new curriculum, which comes into force in 2022, for all children aged from 5 to 16 and will be embedded across the curriculum rather than taught as a separate subject.

[5] The announcement follows a report by Wales's sex and relationships education expert panel, which concluded that SRE was often too biological and too negative, with not enough attention given to rights, gender equity, emotions and relationships.

[6] The announcement was welcomed by charities and campaigners including Stonewall Cymru. The charity's director, Andrew White, was a member of the expert panel and said his charity had lobbied for years for this change.

[7] He said: "It's great news, particularly as this week is the anniversary of the introduction of section 28 and our research shows that a majority of LGBT young people here in Wales have heard nothing about LGBT issues in the classroom.

[8] "The legacy of section 28 unfortunately still lives on and this change will go some way to readdressing the

balance."

⑨ He said it was important that issues were discussed in the classroom. "If we don't, those conversations will happen on the web with sometimes unreliable sources."

⑩ The panel's chair, Emma Renold, a professor of childhood studies at Cardiff University, said the changes would mean sex and the issues surrounding it would not be limited to biology lessons. "It will broaden it out so you can cover the issues in humanities and expressive arts as well as science for example," she said.

⑪ "We identified what constitutes high-quality RSE provision and provided the Welsh government a blueprint because we were calling for a major overhaul. It's not just about curriculum content but about developing the infrastructure, teacher training and support systems that are necessary to ensure it actually works."

⑫ She said the changes were more progressive than in England and could mean Wales would soon be leading the way internationally when it comes to sex education.

⑬ Eleri Butler, the chief executive of Welsh Women's Aid, said the new curriculum was a positive step towards eradicating violence and abuse.

⑭ She said: "It's vital that children and young people learn about age-appropriate relationships and sexuality education, and have access to high-quality learning and support about equality, safety, sexual consent and healthy relationships."

The Keys to Reading Passages

l. 1 …… Wales
イングランド、スコットランドと共にグレート・ブリテンを構成する地域。2008年の調査では、イギリス（グレート・ブリテンおよび北アイルランド連合王国）の人口の5%を占める。イングランドに統合された今もウェールズ語やケルト文化が残っている。

l. 5 …… sexuality
「セクシュアリティ」とは、非常に議論を呼ぶ複雑な概念であるが、単純化をおそれず言えば、性的指向や性的自認を含む、性に関わる身体的行為や表象を総称するもの。対してジェンダー（gender, l. 23）は社会的・文化的役割としての性（差）を指す。

l. 11 …… section 28
1988年、ウェールズ、イングランド、スコットランドで施行された地方自治法。2000年にスコットランドで、2003年にイングランドおよびウェールズで廃止。

l. 12 …… LGBT
LGBTとはレズビアン（lesbian、女性同性愛者）、ゲイ（gay、男性同性愛者）、バイセクシャル（bisexual、両性愛者）、トランスジェンダー（transgender、身体上の性別に違和感を持つ人）の頭文字をとったもの。LGBT+と表記されることもあり、+（plus）にはアセクシャル（asexual、性的欲求や恋愛に興味がない人）やクエスチョニング（Questioning、自分の性的指向や性的自認が定まっていない、あるいは定めたくない人）などLGBT以外の性的マイノリティも含める意図がある。また、規範的な異性愛以外の、LGBTを含むあらゆるセクシャリティを指す概念の「クィア」（queer）があり、クエスチョニングもしくはクィアの頭文字Qを足して、LGBTQもしくはLGBTQ+という言葉も用いられる。

l. 14 …… consent
特にsexual consent（性的同意、l. 61）の意味で、性教育や法整備の場などで議論されるホットなキーワードである。性的な行動を起こす際、相手の同意を得る、あるいはお互いの同意のもと性行為を行なうのは当たり前のようで、実はそう単純ではない。上下関係など利害がからみはっきり拒絶の意思が示せない場合や、酩酊状態など同意能力が疑わしい状態であっても、拒絶の意思を示さなかったから同意があったとしてしまう場合も多い。さらには「イヤよイヤよも好きのうち」（"no means yes"）という神話が根深く、性的な行動を起こす側の解釈と受け手の意思が乖離している場合が少なくない。そのため、性教育の場で「同意」が話題になる時、"yes means yes"と"no means no"が大前提になることが改めて確認される。2018年にはスウェーデンで「明白な同意」のない性行為はレイプとする新法が施行された。また、性的な同意を判断する能力を備えていると見なす年齢を何歳以上にするかという、同意年齢（an age of consent）もしばしば議論の対象になる。

l. 19-20 …… sex and relationships education（SRE）
「性と人間関係の教育」が現行の科目名。RSEに改名されることになった。

l. 25 …… Stonewall Cymru
「ストーンウォール・カムリ支部」。ストーンウォールは1989年、セクション28施行を受け、その廃止に向けてイングランドで設立されたLGBTのための活動団体であり、スコットランド、ウェールズに支部がある。カムリとはウェールズ語で「ウェールズ」の意味である。なお、ストーンウォールとは元々、1969年アメリカ、ニューヨークのゲイバー「ストー

ンウォール・イン」に警察が踏み込んできた際に起きた同性愛者による暴動（抵抗）事件を指す。当時、アメリカでは同性愛が違法とされており、警察によるゲイバーへの踏み込みや同性愛者の拘束が頻繁に行われていたが、同性愛者たちが目立った抵抗をすることがなかった。そのため、ストーンウォール暴動は同性愛者たちが初めて警察に立ち向かった出来事としてLGBTの歴史や文化の中で記念碑的な意味を持つ。

l. 55…… Women's Aid

「ウィメンズエイド」とは、1974年にイギリスで設立された家庭内暴力の被害者の保護支援や、家庭内暴力根絶を目指す団体。

Checking Your Understanding: True or False

本文の内容に照らして合っているものにはTを、間違えているものにはFを書きなさい。

1. RSE will include issues such as consent and respecting diversity.
2. LGBT issues have been discussed in the classroom in Wales.
3. Andrew White was against section 28.
4. LGBT students have access to reliable information about LGBT issues online.

How to Read a Paragraph

以下の問いに答えなさい。なお、（ ）内はヒントとなる段落番号です。

1. セクション28はどのような法律ですか。(Paragraph 3)

2. ウェールズの性と人間関係の専門家委員会の報告書の内容を説明しなさい。(Paragraph 5)

3. 専門家委員会はウェールズ政府にカリキュラムの内容の他に、どのような青写真を提供しましたか。(Paragraph 11)

Translating into English

Reading Passages を見ずに、日本語に合うように（　）内の語句を並び替えて、英文を完成させましょう。冒頭に来る語でも頭文字を小文字にしてあります。

1. 彼は、彼の団体がこの変化を求めて、ロビー活動をしてきたと語った。
(for, said, his, had, change, lobbied, this, charity, he).

_____

2. ウェールズにおけるLGBTの若者の大半は教室内でLGBTの話題について聞いたことがなかった。
A majority of LGBT young people in Wales (about, heard, have, nothing, LGBT, issues) in the classroom.

_____

3. 新しいカリキュラムは暴力と虐待根絶に向けた前向きな一歩である。
The new (a, towards, and, positive, is, eradicating, step, violence, curriculum, abuse).

_____

Listening Summary

CD-13

音声を聴き、[　]内から適切な語を選んで空欄を埋めなさい。

The Welsh government announced an ¹(　　　) of SRE's curriculum. The subject is renamed relationships and sex education (RSE) and will be LGBT ²(　　　). Section 28 banned teaching LGBT issues in schools. Even after abolishing it, the ³(　　　) of section 28 still has been around, so ⁴(　　　) and campaigners like Stonewall Cymru have ⁵(　　　) for a long time for the change. Besides, Eleri Butler, who has fought for ⁶(　　　) violence and domestic ⁷(　　　) welcomes new RSE.

- legacy ● abuse ● lobbied ● overhaul ● charities ● inclusive ● eradicating

Unit 7 Autonomous Cars Likely to Benefit Elderly in Future
自動運転車と高齢者の未来

日本でも高齢者 (the elderly) の運転をめぐる議論がたびたび話題になるが、とりわけ自動車の運転が日常生活を送る上でほぼ必須となっている地方部 (countryside) では、公共交通機関も削減傾向にあり単純に答えが出せる問題ではない。そこで福音となりうるのが自動運転車 (self-driving car) である。将来、自動運転の技術が実用化されれば、高齢や身体的なハンディキャップ (physical limitations) で運転できなかった人が運転できるようになり、より多くの人が自立した生活を送れることが期待されている。自動運転車が実用化される前夜のアメリカの様子を見てみよう。

Matching Words & Phrases

1〜10 までの単語の語義を a〜j のなかから選んで、線で結びなさい。

1. benefit
2. mobility
3. issue [名]
4. virtually
5. postpone
6. forecast
7. penetrate
8. summon
9. in service
10. wear out

a. （定期刊行物の）号（▶「問題」の意味もあり）
b. 先送りにする
c. 呼び出す
d. 予測
e. 磨耗する
f. 移動性、可動性
g. 浸透する
h. 稼働している
i. …の利益になる
j. 実質的に

Reading Passages

1. Self-driving cars will change millions of people's lives for the better by providing independence and mobility to those who can't drive because of physical limitations or age. The technology will allow more people to live on their own terms and participate in what the most of us consider everyday life. "Autonomy promises better mobility and safety for more people at a lower cost," Larry Burns, retired General Motors chief of R&D and strategic planning, writes in the first issue of *Autonomous Vehicle Engineering*, a new publication by the Society of Automotive Engineers.

2. Autonomous vehicles could also lead to greater demand for vehicles, as the population of people who can use them expands from those of driving age to virtually anybody who can use an app. Like phone companies before the iPhone was introduced, automakers are living through the last moments before their industry changes fundamentally and forever.

3. The technology is arriving just in time, said Eric Noble, president of product development consultant The Carlab in Orange, Calif. "Autonomy is good for society. It will extend the time of driving and independent living for the largest generation ever: the baby boom," Mr. Noble said. "The technology aligns perfectly with our demographic needs. Baby boomers had to take the keys when their parents could no longer drive. Autonomy allows them to postpone that moment in their own lives, and extends their working life."

4. Most forecasts say that totally autonomous vehicles won't be widespread until around 2030, but the technology's early steps are already showing what's possible. General Motors' Cadillac Super Cruise does nearly all the driving on limited access highways, where there are no intersections or traffic lights. Self-driving taxi service Voyage operates autonomous Ford

Fusions in the Villages, a retirement community near San Jose, Calif. Real estate developer Bedrock has tested autonomous employee shuttles for employees in downtown Detroit.

5 It's easier to provide autonomy in limited areas like a gated community or around a downtown office area, because there are fewer variables to deal with. "The technology is ideal for areas that are digitally mapped in detail," said Joe Phillippi, principal of Autotrends Consulting. "It will take time for autonomy to penetrate into the deep suburbs and countryside."

6 The way automakers sell and service vehicles will change, too. Ride-sharing, in which people summon a vehicle when they need it, could keep vehicles in service for more hours every day than single-owner personal vehicles.

7 "There's an opportunity for the number of vehicles on the road to stay the same or increase as we open up the number of people who can use them" IHS Markit senior analyst Stephanie Brinley said. Suddenly everybody from a 6-year-old being shuttled to Cub Scouts to my 94-year-old mother is a potential customer. "Cars will be used for more hours every day," Ms. Brinley said. "They'll wear out faster and need repairs and replacement more frequently."

The Keys to Reading Passages・・・・・・・・・・・・・・・・

l. 1 …… self-driving car
「自動運転車」を指す表現は他にも、この Unit のタイトルの autonomous car や autonomous vehicle（l. 10）が使われている。

l. 6 …… autonomy
本来は「自立（性）、自主（性）」を意味するが、自動運転車の文脈である本文では「自動運転」の意味で使われている。autonomous も本文では「自動運転の」という意味になる。

l. 8 …… General Motors
「ゼネラルモーターズ社」は、アメリカの大手自動車メーカー。l. 35 の Ford（フォード・モーター社）も同じくアメリカの大手自動車メーカー。

l. 23 …… the baby boom
「ベビーブーム」の時に生まれたのが (the) baby boomers（ベビーブーム世代）であり、アメリカでは普通 1946 年から 1964 年に生まれた人々を指す。

l. 33 …… limited access highway
アメリカのハイウェイは料金所のない無料の道路も多い。ここで指しているのは日本の高速道路のような料金所のある有料のハイウェイのことである。

l. 38 …… shuttle
定期的に往復するバスのこと。動詞（l. 56）だと「往復させる（する）」の意味になる。

l. 41 …… gated community
「ゲーテッド・コミュニティ」とは、周囲をゲートとフェンスで囲い、住民以外の出入りを制限するため警備員がゲートで人の出入りを監視する高級住宅地。

l. 56 …… Cub Scout
「カブスカウト」はボーイスカウトの年少団員版の組織（だいたい 5 歳から 12 歳までぐらい）。

Checking Your Understanding: True or False

📝 本文の内容に照らして合っているものにはTを、間違えているものにはFを書きなさい。

1. According to Larry Burns, self-driving cars will provide more people with better mobility and safety at a higher cost. ☐

2. Baby boomers are likely to drive a car longer than their parents did. ☐

3. General Motors' Cadillac Super Cruise drives itself everywhere. ☐

4. Self-driving cars will need repairs. ☐

How to Read a Paragraph

📝 以下の問いに答えなさい。なお、（　）内はヒントとなる段落番号です。

1. 自動運転車が実用化されれば、どのような人が自動車メーカーの顧客になり得ますか。(Paragraph 2)

   _____

2. "The technology is arriving just in time" (l. 19) について、エリック・ノーブル氏は何に間に合ったと言っているのですか。(Paragraph 3)

   _____
   _____

3. 現段階で自動運転車はどのような場所での実用に向いていますか。(Paragraph 5)

   _____
   _____

Translating into English

Reading Passages を見ずに、日本語に合うように（　）内の語句を並び替えて、英文を完成させましょう。冒頭に来る語でも頭文字を小文字にしてあります。

1. 自動運転が遠く離れた郊外や田舎にまで浸透するには時間がかかるだろう。
   (the, into, to, for, will, take, penetrate, deep, it, time, autonomy) suburbs and countryside.

2. ライドシェアは一人のオーナーが所有する個人の車よりも、長時間にわたり日々車を稼働させることができるだろう。
   Ride-sharing (for, in, could, keep, more, every day, hours, vehicles, service) than single-owner personal vehicles.

3. 道路を走る自動車の数は現状維持するチャンスがある。
   There's (the, the, an, for, to, of, on the road, same, stay, opportunity, vehicles, number).

Listening Summary

CD-15

音声を聴き、□内から適切な語を選んで空欄を埋めなさい。

Self-driving cars will ¹(　　　) the elderly and those with physical disabilities by providing independence and ²(　　　). If totally autonomous vehicles are ³(　　　), anybody who can use an app will be a ⁴(　　　) customer for automakers. However, most ⁵(　　　) say it will take more time. For now, self-driving cars are in ⁶(　　　) within limited areas where there are fewer variables to deal with. Besides, the autonomous technology is suitable to areas that are digitally ⁷(　　　) in detail.

- benefit
- potential
- widespread
- mobility
- mapped
- forecasts
- service

Unit 8

Millennials Go Minimal
ミレニアル世代のミニマルな消費傾向

1981-1996年生まれのミレニアル世代及びそれに続く世代がアメリカの労働人口 (workforce) をかなりの割合で占めるようになり、彼らのライフスタイルや消費傾向が今後の社会・経済動向を決める大きな鍵を握るようになってきた。不況のなかに育ち、多額の学生ローン (student debt) を返済しながら低迷する求人市場 (struggling job market) で職を求め働くミレニアル世代の志向にぴったりとフィットするのがミニマリズムと呼ばれるライフスタイルなのだ。シェアリング経済 (Unit 2) やサブスクリプション経済 (Unit 13) と並んで、ここでも「モノの所有」への関心が薄れていることがうかがえる。

Matching Words & Phrases

1〜10までの単語の語義をa〜jのなかから選んで、線で結びなさい。

1. inspire O to do
2. donate
3. entrepreneur
4. recession
5. pay off
6. (be) adept at...
7. would rather
8. disposable
9. available
10. (be) comprised of...

a. 不況、不景気
b. 意欲を与えて…させる
c. 寄付する
d. …から成っている
e. 自由に使える
f. 利用できる
g. …に精通している
h. 完済する
i. …する方が良い
j. 起業家

Reading Passages

[1] Marie Kondo's book, *The Life-Changing Magic of Tidying Up: The Japanese Art of Decluttering and Organizing*, brought minimalism to the mainstream. Although it is not a new concept, the minimalist lifestyle is trending across the United States. The movement has inspired people to move into tiny homes, cut their wardrobes and donate their possessions. Countless bloggers document their forays into minimalism and even the television channel, HGTV, has taken to highlighting the benefits and has three shows on tiny houses in its current lineup. Many entrepreneurs have picked up on this and are figuring out how they can capitalize on the minimalism and decluttering trends.

[2] Millennials in particular are seeking out this minimalist lifestyle. Millennials—the 18-34 demographic make up more than a quarter of the U.S. population and the majority of the workforce. Millennials have a unique set of values around how they choose to spend their money. They grew up during the recession, entered a struggling job market and must now pay off record amounts of student debt. Retail expert, Robin Lewis, of The Robin Report, explained the consequences of millennial factors, "This is a generation that is bigger than the boomers in population, but their wallets are smaller, and they are more into the style of life than the stuff of life. This is a big threat to retail. They're not into a lot of shopping."

[3] Millennials are highly adept at using technology and social media influences many of their purchases. They prefer to spend on experiences rather than on stuff. Seventy-eight percent of millennials—compared to 59% of baby boomers—"would rather pay for an experience than material goods," according to a survey from Harris Poll and Eventbrite cited on Bloomberg. They favor products marketed as ethical, sustainable and

environmentally friendly.

④ At Fung Global Retail & Technology, we believe the minimalism and decluttering movements will stick around for some time. Even as millennials pay off their debt and garner more disposable income, we believe they will choose to spend their money on experiences—such as traveling, concerts and eating out—rather than things.

⑤ Other industry trends support this idea. The sharing economy, in which consumers choose to use the new set of services available through Uber and Airbnb rather than buy cars or time shares, and the caring economy, comprised of consumers who spend on ethical and sustainable brands, are two examples. We predict companies that provide consumers, particularly millennials, with services that fit into this minimalist and socially conscious lifestyle will see success.

The Keys to Reading Passages

l. 1 …… Marie Kondo
「近藤麻理恵」は片付けコンサルタント。2010年出版の『人生がときめく片づけの魔法』が大ベストセラーになる。また、本文にあるアメリカ版タイトルもベストセラーとなり、2015年にはタイム誌の「最も影響力がある100人」に選出された。

l. 3 …… minimalism
必要最低限までモノの所有を切り詰めるライフスタイルを指す。その方法や程度、信念については諸々あるが、「断捨離」もその一つだと考えられている。また、このライフスタイルを実践する人をミニマリスト (minimalist) と呼ぶ。

l. 14 …… Millennials
諸説あるようだが、通常ミレニアル世代は1981-1996年生まれとされることが多い。それ以降はポストミレニアル世代 (Post-Millennials) として、Generation Z や iGen と呼ばれることが多い。

l. 15 …… the 18-34 demographic
記事執筆の2016年当時に18-34歳 (すなわち、1997-1981年生まれ) をミレニアル世代と定義づけているが、より正確には Millennials の項を参照。

l. 35 …… ethical
「倫理にかなった、エシカルな」。近頃、経済活動の文脈で使われるキーワードである ethical とは、製品の生産販売過程で低賃金による労働者の搾取や児童労働、環境破壊、動物実験など倫理にかなわないことを行なっていないことを指している。例えば、フェアトレードなどは ethical だと言える。

l. 35 …… sustainable
「環境を壊さず利用可能な、継続維持できる、サステナブルな」。ethical と同様に経済活動や環境を考える文脈でキーワードとなっている語。元々の意味は「継続維持できる」であるが、経済成長と引き換えに引き起こされた天然資源の枯渇や環境汚染など、地球環境や人間社会のシステムや文明そのものの「維持」が危ぶまれている近年、それらを「継続維持できる」ような経済活動が生活様式を形容するものとして使われている。したがって、「地球に優しい」などの訳語が当てられることもある。

l. 37 …… Fung Global Retail & Technology, we believe...
Fung Global Retail & Technology は本文の筆者が業務執行取締役を務めていたシンクタンク。ここで急に "we" が出てくるのは、筆者も含めた会社の分析を述べているからである。

l. 47 …… time share
「タイムシェア (共同使用権)」とは、複数の人々が期間を区切って使用する目的でリゾートマンションやホテルなどの利用権を購入することであるが、シェアリング経済の想定するシェアの形態と違うのは、同じ物件を継続的に利用するため、「所有」に近い点である。

l. 47-48 …… the caring economy
「ケアリング経済」とは、人々や自然に対する思いやりが最優先事項となる経済システム。

Checking Your Understanding: True or False

本文の内容に照らして合っているものにはTを、間違えているものにはFを書きなさい。

1. Many entrepreneurs see the minimalism and decluttering trends as opportunities to make a fortune.

2. The baby boomers grew up during the recession.

3. After they pay off their student debt, Millennials will buy more stuff.

4. Millennials tend to be socially conscious.

How to Read a Paragraph

以下の問いに答えなさい。なお、（ ）内はヒントとなる段落番号です。

1. ミニマリズムのライフスタイルの具体例を Paragraph 1 より挙げなさい。

   _____
   _____

2. ミレニアル世代はベビーブーム世代に比べてどのような傾向がありますか。(Paragraphs 2 & 3)

   _____
   _____

3. ミレニアル世代はモノを購入する際、どのようなものを選ぶ傾向がありますか。(Paragraph 3)

   _____
   _____

Translating into English

Reading Passages を見ずに、日本語に合うように（　）内の語句を並び替えて、英文を完成させましょう。冒頭に来る語でも頭文字を小文字にしてあります。

1. ミレニアル世代、すなわち 18-34 歳の層は、アメリカの人口の四分の一以上を構成している。
   Millennials—the 18-34 demographic (a, of, up, more, than, make, the U.S. population, quarter).

   _____

2. 彼らはたくさんモノを買うのが好きではないのだ。
   (a, of, into, are, not, shopping, lot, they).

   _____

3. ケアリング経済は、倫理にかなった、環境を壊さず利用可能な製品にお金を費やす消費者から成っている。
   The caring economy (on, of, and, ethical, sustainable, is, spend, comprised, who, consumers, brands).

   _____

Listening Summary

音声を聴き、□内から適切な語を選んで空欄を埋めなさい。

Millennials ¹(　　　　) the minimalist and socially conscious lifestyle. They experienced the ²(　　　　), entered a struggling job market and have huge amounts of student debt to ³(　　　　). Millennials, ⁴(　　　　) to the baby boomers, ⁵(　　　　) pay for an experience than material goods. Besides, they choose to spend on ethical and ⁶(　　　　) products. Companies that provide consumers with services that ⁷(　　　　) this lifestyle will see success.

- seek out
- pay off
- would rather
- sustainable
- fit into
- recession
- compared

Special Unit

Namie Amuro, "The Madonna of Japan," Is Retiring, But Her Style Influence Lives on

時代とリンクし続けた安室奈美恵

「シェアリング経済」(Unit 2) や「ミレニアル世代のミニマリズム的消費傾向」(Unit 8)、「サブスクリプション経済」(Unit 13) のいずれの角度からも見えてくるのが「モノの所有ばなれ」と「消費スタイルの変化」である。日本では戦後、人々はモノの所有・大量消費へと駆り立てられていった。音楽において、CD の売り上げが最高潮を迎えたのが小室サウンド全盛の 1990 年代、安室奈美恵が小室哲哉プロデュースのもと個人名義でミリオンヒットを連発していた頃である。1997 年 2 月リリースの「CAN YOU CELEBRATE?」は 229.6 万枚を売り上げ、オリコン歴代女性シングル売上 1 位を占めている。また、10 代の安室は、茶髪、日焼けした肌 (tan skin)、ミニスカート、厚底のミリタリーブーツ (platform combat boots) といったその服装 (outfit) を真似た (emulate)「アムラー」と呼ばれる大勢の (a legion of) 若い女性を生み出し (spawn) 社会現象となった。

2018 年 9 月 16 日に引退した安室奈美恵。
台湾の歌手ジョリン・ツァイ (Jolin Tsai) のワールドツアーコンサートで。
Photo © VCG/VCG via Getty Images

しかし、2000 年代以降音楽業界全般で CD が売れなくなり、安室の CD 売り上げもかつての勢いはなくなった。しかし、安室は早々に小室のプロデュースを離れ、活動の重点を MC なしのライブに移し、モノ消費 (CD 販売) から体験消費 (ライブ) へと売り方を変え、20 代、30 代と歌姫の地位を維持し続けた。

一方、一連の引退セレモニーではライブの活況はもちろん、DVD や CD についてはミリオンやダブルミリオンを連発することになった。これは所有ばなれや消費のスタイルの変化を否定する現象なのか、それとも 90 年代の一時のノスタルジックなリバイバルなのか？ はたまた、どちらとも違う未来の予兆なのか？

また、神話化された歌姫の引退と言えば、結婚を機に引退した山口百恵が思い出されるが、安室は人気絶頂の 19 歳の頃、TRF のダンサーのサムと結婚し（のちに離婚）子育てをしながらキャリアを築き、一般的に子育てが一段落したと言われる段階で引退し別の生き方をすることを決めた。安室奈美恵という存在は、これからの（女性）人生のあり方を占う存在でもあるのだろうか――。

Reading Passages

[1] The golden rule of stardom is always leave your audience wanting more, and no one understands that better than Japanese music star Namie Amuro. Dubbed the Madonna of Japan, Amuro has been making hits
5 since the mid-'90s, delivering a provocative, hip-hop-influenced sound that has proven influential. She has been the reigning queen of the J-pop scene for 25 years, inspiring both the music and the style of the acts that followed her. In a business defined by its revolving
10 door of teenage talent, she is one of a few performers to successfully make the transition from girl group member to solo act and maintain her relevance for decades. Amuro has created songs that have become iconic—her track "Can You Celebrate?" remains the top-selling
15 Japanese single by a solo artist more than 20 years after its release—while cultivating an image as a rule-breaker, which makes her latest move all the more fascinating. This past September, on the eve of her 40th birthday, she announced that she'd be stepping away from public life.

20 [2] The impact of Amuro's retirement on the music industry is clear. But her songs aren't the only important aspect of her legacy. Amuro's influence in the world of fashion was every bit as interesting. She dabbled in modeling after debuting as part of girl group Super
25 Monkey's back in 1992, and her confidence in front of the camera brought her the attention that would eventually propel her to the position of group leader. When the group rebranded itself as Namie Amuro with Super Monkey's, it was clear that she was stealing a page
30 from Diana Ross's playbook. By the time she went solo with "Body Feels Exit" in 1995, Amuro had established herself as an alternative to the typical idol. She spawned the "Amuraa" style, a look focused on tan skin, short skirts, and platform combat boots, inspiring a legion of
35 fans who emulated her every outfit. Avoiding the cutesy

school girl looks favored by her contemporaries, Amuro instead sought out pieces that were daring. In an era when idols weren't yet clad in head-to-toe designer looks, she was influenced by the runways, frequently wearing pieces from Chanel and Versace. She also embraced the bling-y luxury aesthetic of '90s hip-hop videos, helping to popularize the oversized streetwear look in Japan.

3 Amuro often challenged Japanese social mores by simply living her life. When she decided to get tattoos in honor of her son and mother, her much-discussed body art broke with tradition. As she was one of the only women in J-pop to sport prominent ink, it was a bold statement. Likewise her status as a performer over the age of 30 who fearlessly sports sexier styles, such as ruffled mini-skirts, corsetry, and thigh-high boots, made her an anomaly within the teen-focused music scene.

4 Amuro's influence on fashion is certainly clear at the shows of Tokyo Fashion Week, which are currently in full swing. Labels including DressedUndressed and HARE are doubling down on the elevated streetwear and cool '90s fashion trends she pioneered. While it has become common for musicians to "retire" only to return shortly thereafter—Jay-Z, Justin Bieber, and Lauryn Hill have all stepped away from music at one point—Amuro has made her intentions clear. Updating her social media with the equivalent of a two weeks notice letter, she gave fans an end date—September 16, 2018—while thanking them for their years of devotion. With a final tour set for early next year, it's likely that there are still a few great fashion moments in her future, but the legacy she's created will live on long after she's sung her last tune.

The Keys to Reading Passages

l. 4…… the Madonna of Japan
「日本のマドンナ」。アメリカの歌手マドンナ（1958年−）は、過激なファッションや発言、行動で様々なタブーに挑戦し続けてきた。

l. 24-25…… Super Monkey's
沖縄アクターズスクールの5人で結成されたグループ。1994年7月より「安室奈美恵 with SUPER MONKEY'S」になった。安室もソロ活動が多くなり、また安室以外のメンバーは MAX としてブレイクし、1996年9月に活動休止。

l. 29-30…… it was clear that ... Diana Ross's playbook.
「彼女がダイアナ・ロスの作戦帳から1ページを盗んでいるのは明らかだった。」 ダイアナ・ロス（1944年−）はアメリカの歌手で、ブラックミュージック界のレジェンド。1960年代にシュプリームス（Supremes）という黒人女性ボーカルトリオでデビューし、ソウルミュージックのモータウンレコードからヒットを連発した。ロスは1969年にシュプリームスを脱退し、ソロ歌手として大成功を収め今に至る（一方、他のメンバーはその後、成功しなかった）。安室のSUPER MONKEY'Sでの活動とのちのソロ活動にロスの軌跡を重ねてみよう。

l. 31…… "Body Feels Exit"
1995年5月リリースの小室哲哉が初めてプロデュースしたシングルのタイトル。安室奈美恵の単独名義で発表。88.2万枚を売り上げた。

l. 39…… runway
「（ショーのモデルが歩く）ステージ、ランウェイ」。比喩的にランウェイでコレクションを発表するハイブランドのデザイナーのファッションを指している。

l. 40…… Chanel and Versace
「シャネルとヴェルサス（ヴェルサーチのカジュアルな若者向けのライン）」はいずれもラグジュアリーなハイブランド。

l. 41…… bling-y
bling（派手な、見せびらかすための）に「…の（ような）性質を持つ」という意味の接尾語"-y"をつけた言葉。大きなダイヤや金の指輪やネックレスを誇らしげにつけたヒップホッパーを想像してほしい。

l. 53…… Tokyo Fashion Week
パリ、ミラノ、ロンドン、ニューヨークの世界四大ファッションショーの次に位置付けられるファッションショー。ファッションショーをコレクションと呼ぶのは日本だけで、英語では"fashion week"と称する。

l. 61…… equivalent of a two weeks notice letter
「2週間前退職予告期間通知と同等のもの」。日本だと退職する30日前に書面で予告する必要があるが、アメリカではその期間が2週間である。ここでは、一般的な「退職予告」に安室の「引退予告」が喩えられている。

Pair/Group Work

Q1. 安室が、1990年代的なテレビへの露出でCDを売るスタイルから、ライブ重視のスタイルへと早々に転換を図ったことや、ファッションも含めた（ライフ）スタイルでファンをひきつけたことは、Unit 8のミレニアル世代のミニマルな消費傾向を先取りしたものと言えるでしょうか。

Q2. 2017年から2018年にかけての一連の引退セレモニーのなかで、安室のDVDやCDがミリオンやダブルミリオンを連発したのは、1990年代のノスタルジー的なリバイバルなのか、あるいは所有ばなれの流れを否定する動きなのか、それとも他の未来を占う現象なのでしょうか。

Q3. 近頃のディズニープリンセスの映画でも王子様（的な存在）との結婚がゴールではなくなってきているようです。一般的に言って子育てが一段落したタイミングでの、そして40歳での安室の引退は、どのような点で女性の生き方やキャリアのあり方を占う出来事だと言えそうでしょうか。

Unit 9 Esports-FIFA's eWorld Cup Catching Up with the Real Thing

本家に迫る FIFA e ワールドカップ

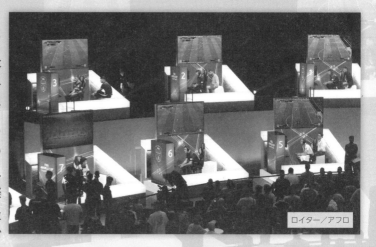

eスポーツ (esports) とはエレクトロニック・スポーツ (electronic sports) の略で、複数のプレーヤーが参加するビデオゲーム上の対戦をスポーツ競技とみなす表現である。オリンピックの正式競技になるかもしれないとのニュースを耳にした人も多いと思うが、すでに FIFA (国際サッカー連盟) と世界的なゲーム会社である EA スポーツ (EA sports) が共催する、e ワールドカップ (eWorld Cup) が開催されている。そこでは、FIFA 公認のビデオゲームで競技が行われる。ドーピング検査 (dope test) や賭け事の監視 (monitoring of betting) などが導入された 2018 年の大会では、ますますホンモノのワールドカップに近づきつつある。現状や今後の課題、見通しなどを見てみよう。

Matching Words & Phrases

1〜10 までの単語の語義を a〜j のなかから選んで、線で結びなさい。

1. involve
2. agent
3. (be) affiliated with...
4. measure
5. stand out (from...)
6. room
7. note [動]
8. regulation
9. in that respect
10. mature

a. 代理人
b. 余地
c. …と提携している
d. その点では
e. 伴う
f. 言及する
g. 成熟する
h. (…より) 卓越する、抜きん出る
i. 規則
j. 手段

Reading Passages

[1] LONDON — FIFA's eWorld Cup may not actually involve kicking a ball through any real goalposts but the virtual game is catching up fast with the club professionals.

[2] Random dope tests and the monitoring of betting trends are a new feature of this weekend's tournament in London, while professional coaches and even player agents are becoming a reality.

[3] Some U.S. universities now offer esports scholarships while many of the top players are affiliated with big name European clubs and earning good money. Saturday's eWorld Cup winner will take home $250,000 (192,204.20 pounds).

[4] Jean-François Pathy, director of marketing services for world body FIFA, told Reuters on Friday that the trend was set to continue and this year's tournament was 'year one' of a new model.

[5] "On the prize money, I don't really see a big move in the near future. What is going to change is the sport becoming more professional," he said as group stages came to a conclusion at the O2 Arena. "The first steps this year were anti-doping measures, gambling and betting monitoring."

[6] The players are emerging as personalities in their own rights, watched by a global audience online that is growing rapidly, and doing interviews in a roped-off media mixed zone.

[7] The 32 finalists have had to stand out from a crowd of 20 million who entered worldwide on Xbox and PlayStation, and with an estimated 80 million players of the FIFA game there is plenty of room for growth. The EA Sports FIFA Twitter feed counts 6.35 million followers, compared to FIFA's 12.1 million.

[8] "The challenge is to find a structure that fits this huge number (of participants). You need to make sure

everyone's got a fair chance at it," said Pathy.

⑨ "But yes, we expect growth in the territories we're in at the moment, we're not really touching on Asia yet. That's an area where we need to go to. It will grow for sure, by how much we don't know yet." "We've seen in the last three years already an enormous jump year-on-year."

⑩ Pathy would not give any figures on projected revenues, other than saying the eWorld Cup was "not a money maker right now" but noted that some analysts had for some time presented esports as the next $1 billion industry.

⑪ "It's good to have a structure, it is good to have agents, players, regulations. This year we've got a kit regulation for the first time like at the FIFA World Cup where you can put your sponsors but in a very formal way," he said.

⑫ "It will replicate the normal football business for sure. The last year, or year-and-a-half, we've seen a big jump in that respect with clubs and leagues getting involved, sponsorship deals coming in. The media rights will grow as well," he added. "It is maturing. I think it will become more and more similar to real football, if you call it like that."

The Keys to Reading Passages ················

l. 1 ····· FIFA's eWorld Cup
2004年からFIFA Interactive World Cupの名前で開催されてきたが、2018年に規模を拡大して名称を変更。

l. 6 ····· this weekend's tournament
2018年8月4日に行われたFIFA eワールドカップの決勝トーナメントを指している。記事はその前日の8月3日に書かれた。

l. 20 ····· group stage
「グループステージ」とは、全チームを数グループに分け各グループでリーグ戦を行なうステージのこと。グループステージ上位のチームは決勝トーナメントに進める。

l. 22-23 ····· gambling and betting
両者とも「賭け事」を表す語として同義で使われることもあるが、厳密にはgamblingは完全に運任せのリスクの高い行為であり、中毒性が心配され政府がしばしば規制の対象にする行為である。それに対して、bettingは結果を予測して賭ける行為であり、二者(賭ける側と請け負う側)の同意に基づいて行われる。また、社会通念を逸脱しない範囲にとどまる行為と見なされている。

l. 24-27 ····· The players...zone.
ここで"are emerging"、"(are) doing"と現在進行形になっているのは、すでに決定しており準備がなされている未来を表す時に使われる現在進行形の用法だからである。つまり、決勝戦でそうすることが決まっていることについて話しているのだ。

l. 27 ····· mixed zone
メディアが試合直後の選手にインタビューをするための、競技会場に用意された取材用のスペース。

l. 29-30 ····· Xbox and PlayStation
「エックスボックス」も「プレイステーション」も家庭用ゲーム機であり、前者はマイクロソフト社、後者はソニーが販売。FIFA eワールドカップはどちらのゲーム機を用いても参加できる。

Checking Your Understanding: True or False

本文の内容に照らして合っているものには T を、間違えているものには F を書きなさい。

1. Every esports player has professional coaches and agents. ☐
2. The prize money will stay the same in the near future. ☐
3. FIFA tweeter feed counts about twice as many as the EA Sports FIFA's. ☐
4. Esports is a $1 billion industry. ☐

How to Read a Paragraph

以下の問いに答えなさい。なお、（ ）内はヒントとなる段落番号です。

1. 2018 年の e ワールドカップでは、本物のサッカーに近づくためにルール面においてどのようなことを導入しましたか。(**Paragraphs 2 & 5**)

   _____

   _____

2. ペイシー氏によれば、e ワールドカップのこれからもっとも成長しそうな余地はどこにありますか。(**Paragraph 9**)

   _____

   _____

3. ビジネスに関して、ペイシー氏はどのような点で e ワールドカップは本物のサッカーに近づきつつあると言っていますか。(**Paragraph 12**)

   _____

   _____

Translating into English

Reading Passages を見ずに、日本語に合うように（　）内の語句を並び替えて、英文を完成させましょう。冒頭に来る語でも頭文字を小文字にしてあります。

1. アメリカの大学のなかには今ではeスポーツに奨学金を出すところもある一方で、トッププレイヤーの多くが有名なヨーロッパのクラブと提携し、かなりの額を稼いでいる。

   Some U.S. universities now (the, of, with, while, top, big, many, European, are, offer, affiliated, name, scholarships, players, clubs, esports) and earning good money.

   _____

2. 変化していくことは、そのスポーツがよりプロ化することである。

   What (the, to, professional, more, is, is, change, becoming, going, sport).

   _____

3. 課題はこの膨大な参加者の数に適した仕組みを見つけることである。

   The challenge (a, this, that, to, of, huge, is, fits, find, participants, structure, number).

   _____

Listening Summary

CD-20

音声を聴き、　　　内から適切な語を選んで空欄を埋めなさい。

FIFA's eWorld Cup is rapidly ¹(　　　　) up with real professional football, although it may not actually ²(　　　　) kicking a real ball. It introduced anti-doping ³(　　　　) and gambling and betting monitoring for the first time in 2018. In addition, it established ⁴(　　　　) on sponsorship deals like FIFA World Cup. FIFA's eWorld Cup is not a money maker right now but there is plenty of ⁵(　　　　) for growth. Some analysts say esports will be the next $1 ⁶(　　　　) industry. FIFA's eWorld Cup is ⁷(　　　　).

- involve
- measures
- billion
- regulations
- room
- catching
- maturing

58

Unit 10 Is 'Snapchat Dysmorphia' Really Something to Be Worried About?

加工自撮り画像と理想の自分とのギャップ

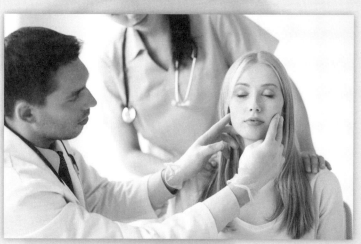

今どきは、美容整形手術 (cosmetic surgery) を受けるときに芸能人の写真ではなく、画像加工した自撮り写真 (filtered selfie) を参考に持ってくる人が多いそうである。スマートフォンがあれば誰でも簡単に画像加工ができるようになった今、自撮り写真のなかに完璧な理想の自分を作り出すことは容易である。さらにそれらの画像加工された自撮りをインスタグラムなどのソーシャルメディアにあげれば、完璧な理想の自分は社会のなかで流通するが、現実の自分との乖離は増すばかりである。その当然の帰結 (consequence) として指摘され始めたスナップチャット醜形恐怖症 (Snapchat dysmorphia) とは。

Matching Words & Phrases

1〜10までの単語の語義をa〜jのなかから選んで、線で結びなさい。

1. pervasiveness
2. unattainable
3. blur
4. certified
5. diagnosis
6. concerned
7. advent
8. self esteem
9. trigger
10. defect

a. 診断
b. 到来
c. 公認された
d. 欠点、欠陥
e. 引き金、誘因
f. 広がり、普及
g. 及ばない、到達不可能な
h. (名詞の後ろに置いて) 当該の、関係している
i. ぼやけさせる
j. 自尊心

Reading Passages

[1] Ever heard of "Snapchat dysmorphia?" The term resurfaced on social media this week when *The Journal of the American Medical Association* published a report raising concerns about the pervasiveness of filtered photographs on smartphones, particularly so-called selfies, and the effects on people's self-perception. "This is an alarming trend because those filtered selfies often present an unattainable look and are blurring the line of reality and fantasy," the article says.

[2] Filtered selfies are self-portrait photos taken on a smartphone using technology that make one's face look more flawless, including features like longer eyelashes or enhanced cheek bones.

[3] It's not a certified medical diagnosis, but the term has been used by some plastic surgeons to describe a consequence of the smartphone era. Dr. Tijion Esho, a cosmetic doctor at The Esho Clinic UK, is said to have coined the term which stems from an uptick in the use of filtered photos as inspiration for cosmetic surgery or treatment.

[4] A 2017 survey by the American Academy of Facial Plastic and Reconstructive Surgery found that 55 percent of surgeons saw patients who want to look better in selfies in their practices — up 13 percent from the previous year.

[5] Esho says it's common to see these selfies used as a reference point, but if it becomes how people see themselves or they want to look exactly like the image, that's when there are concerns.

[6] "Not only is this unrealistic, it's potentially a sign of underlying problems with the patient concerned," he told the BBC. "Further questions should be asked to screen for any element of body dysmorphia. Treating patients that do show those red flags is not only unethical, but also detrimental to the patient, as they need something

that no needle or scalpel can ever provide."

7 The term "Snapchat dysmorphia" is being used to address the rise of plastic surgery tied to filtered images. Experts at Boston University of Medicine's dermatology department published an article this week exploring how filters and edits have altered people's perception of beauty.

8 "The advent and popularity of image-based social media have put Photoshop and filters in everyone's arsenal," the article by members of the Boston University of Medicine's dermatology department says. "The pervasiveness of these filtered images can take a hold on one's self esteem, make one feel inadequate for not looking a certain way in the real world, and may even act as a trigger and lead to body dysmorphic disorder."

9 Body dysmorphic disorder is "a mental disorder in which you can't stop thinking about one or more perceived defects or flaws in your appearance — a flaw that, to others, is either minor or not observable" according to Mayo Clinic. The disorder may cause a person to seek out cosmetic procedures and has been linked to eating disorders and depression.

10 Body dysmorphic disorder hasn't been tied to apps like Snapchat or its competitor Instagram by any research, but it's a topic these researchers feel clinicians should be aware of going forward, especially among young people.

The Keys to Reading Passages

l. 1 …… Snapchat
写真や動画が共有できるSNSアプリ。日本でもおなじみのインスタグラム（l. 59：Instagram）と同種のアプリである。

l. 1 …… dysmorphia
正式名称はbody dysmorphic disorder（身体醜形恐怖症）。客観的には問題がないのに、主観的に自分の身体（の一部）を醜いと思い込み、外見に過剰にとらわれ、生活に支障をきたす疾患のこと。自尊心（self-esteem）の低さとも関わりがあると言われている。

l. 21-22 …… the American Academy of Facial Plastic and Reconstructive Surgery
「全米顔面形成再建外科学会」

l. 27 …… how
この場合、名詞節を導くthat（…ということ、…である次第）と同じ役割をする。ex. It is funny how he said that.（彼がそんなことを言ったなんておかしいこともあるものだ。）／He told me how he had read it in the newspaper.（彼は新聞で読んだと私に言った。）

Checking Your Understanding: True or False

📝 本文の内容に照らして合っているものにはTを、間違えているものにはFを書きなさい。

1. Body dysmorphic disorder is not a certified medical diagnosis. ☐

2. Dr. Esho is said to be the first person to use the term "Snapchat dysmorphia." ☐

3. The pervasiveness of filtered selfies may serve as a trigger and lead to body dysmorphic disorder. ☐

4. Many researchers have tied body dysmorphic disorder to apps like Snapchat. ☐

How to Read a Paragraph

📝 以下の問いに答えなさい。なお、（　）内はヒントとなる段落番号です。

1. 加工を施した自撮り写真の広がりが危険と考えられるのはなぜですか。(Paragraph 1)

   _____

   _____

2. エショ医師は、自撮り写真通りに整形してくれと患者に言われた場合、どうするべきだと言っていますか。(Paragraph 6)

   _____

   _____

3. 身体醜形恐怖症を患うと、本人の主観と客観の間にどのようなズレが生じますか。(Paragraph 9)

   _____

   _____

Translating into English

📝 Reading Passages を見ずに、日本語に合うように（　）内の語句を並び替えて、英文を完成させましょう。冒頭に来る語でも頭文字を小文字にしてあります。

1. 加工した自撮りとは、人の顔をより完璧に仕上げるテクノロジーを使ってスマートフォンで撮られたセルフ・ポートレート写真である。

   Filtered selfies (a, on, that, are, taken, using, make, self-portrait photos, technology, one's face look, smartphone) more flawless.

   _____

2. エショ医師はその言葉を造語したと言われている。

   (to, the, coined, said, is, have, Dr. Esho, term).

   _____

3. 画像ベースのソーシャルメディアが到来し人気を博したおかげでフォトショップと加工技術はみんなの兵器になったのである。

   (the, of, and, image-based, advent, popularity, social media) (have, Photoshop, put, and, filters) in everyone's arsenal.

   _____

Listening Summary

🎧 CD-22

📝 音声を聴き、□内から適切な語を選んで空欄を埋めなさい。

Although it is not a ¹(　　　) medical ²(　　　), the term "Snapchat dysmorphia" has been used to describe a ³(　　　) of the smartphone era, when people, especially young people, see or want to look exactly like a ⁴(　　　) version of themselves in filtered selfies and seek out cosmetic surgery or treatment. It may be a sign of ⁵(　　　) mental health problems with the patient ⁶(　　　). Dr. Esho recommends further questions to be asked to ⁷(　　　) for any symptoms of body dysmorphic disorder.

- concerned
- flawless
- consequence
- certified
- diagnosis
- underlying
- screen

Unit 11 Ending Food Ignorance: Education Is Too Important to Leave to Big Food
子供たちの食育を誰が担うか

Unit 5でアメリカにおける肥満のまん延を見てきたが、子供たちも例外ではない。栄養価の少ない安価で手軽なジャンクフードが溢れる現代社会において、何を食べるか主体的に選ぶことは想像以上に困難である。そもそも、選択の土台となる食の知識や情報を学ぶ機会が家庭や学校でもほとんどない子供たちが多いことは想像に難くない。多くの子どもたちにとって、食の情報はテレビから流れるジャンクフードの宣伝から得るものだったりする。そこで鍵となるのは、やはり学校での食育 (food education or nutrition education) である。食育の担い手が、肥満の連鎖を食い止めるか否かだけでなく、多方面にわたり未来を決めるのかもしれない。

Matching Words & Phrases

1～10までの単語の語義をa～jのなかから選んで、線で結びなさい。

1. underway
2. massive
3. effort
4. initiative
5. outraged
6. trim
7. appreciate
8. ingredient
9. call on
10. if ever

a. 成分、原料
b. 呼びかける、求める
c. 新たな取り組み、新規構想
d. 進行中の（で）
e. 十分理解する（▶多義語で「賞賛する」、「感謝する」などの意味もあり）
f. 大規模の
g. 削減する
h. 仮にあるとすれば
i. 取り組み、試み（▶「努力」という意味もあり）
j. 激怒した

Reading Passages

[1] Would you be surprised to know that there is a highly-sophisticated, multi-billion-dollar campaign underway designed to teach your children about food? There is. In fact, experts agree that this campaign is wildly successful. Unfortunately, the massive instructional campaign to which I refer is the $2 billion effort by the food industry to teach children and teens to want candy, sugar drinks, sugary cereals, and other highly-processed junk foods. Mostly, these lessons are delivered through your television set.

[2] When one-third of American kids are overweight or obese, and are on track to have shorter lives than their parents, it's clear that food education is too important to leave to Big Food. That's why Jamie Oliver's Food Foundation and the organizers behind Food Day (Oct. 24) are collaborating on a new national initiative to put food education in every school.

[3] Parents would be outraged if their children in elementary school didn't learn that two plus two is four. Yet, as Oliver demonstrated in 2010, some American school kids cannot identify tomatoes, beets, or cauliflower, or might mistake an eggplant for a pear!

[4] The anti-hunger group Feeding America estimates that elementary school students receive just 3.4 hours of nutrition education — actual education and not marketing — each year. Fewer than 25 percent of high school students take any family and consumer science classes, formerly known as home economics, and those classes are often the first to go when school budgets are trimmed. And parents have to shoulder some of the blame, when "cooking" actually means "microwaving" or otherwise heating some well-preserved, factory-extruded, combination of flour, fat, salt, sugar, dyes, and other chemicals.

[5] But just as we expect our schools to do the heavy

lifting when it comes to teaching geography, algebra, physical education, and history, we should expect schools to teach children about food — where it comes from and how it affects our bodies and our health. Where it's been done well, we know it works. First of all, most kids find that cooking is fun. The more children cook and prepare fresh recipes from scratch, the more likely they are to appreciate healthier and varied ingredients and develop a skill that will serve them well throughout their lives. The more children learn about food and nutrition, the more likely they are to eat fruits, vegetables, and other healthful foods.

6 We call on policymakers at all levels of government to put food education back in every school. We can't raise another generation of kids that can't tell tomatoes from potatoes, or for whom cooking means pressing the "start" button on the microwave. Let's put food education back in schools because we value our children and their prospects for long, healthy, and happy lives.

7 It will be many years, if ever, before America's real food educators have the same financial resources as America's junk-food manufacturers. But we shouldn't leave the critical task of teaching nutrition to the food industry any more than we'd leave teaching science to the Flat Earth Society.

The Keys to Reading Passages

l. 14……Jamie Oliver

「ジェイミー・オリヴァー」(1975-) は、イギリスのシェフで自身の料理番組を持つ一方、イギリスの公立学校で給食改善運動に取り組んだり、アメリカ各地を回り食育改革を啓蒙し、その様子がTV番組となるなど食育の活動家でもある。(日本でも彼の番組は放映・DVD販売がされている。) また、2010年に"TED Prize"(講演会TEDが選ぶその年の最優秀なスピーチに送られる賞) を受賞した際に"Teach Every Child about Food"というタイトルで受賞講演を行った。なお、本文中の"(Jamie Oliver) Food Foundation"(ジェイミー・オリヴァー・フード・ファウンデーション) は食育を通して健康や幸福を高め、食習慣由来の病気を減らすことを目的としている慈善団体である。

l. 15……Food Day

「フードデー」は、毎年10月24日、アメリカ各地で食について考えるイベントが開催される日である。

l. 20……as Oliver demonstrated in 2010

ジェイミー・オリヴァーは、アメリカのABCテレビの番組"Jamie Oliver's Food Revolution"(2010-11) で、肥満が最も深刻な都市の一つであるアメリカ・ウェストバージニア州のハンティントンに訪れ、住民の食習慣を改善しようと取り組んだ。本文ではその時の様子が描かれている。なお、この番組は優れたテレビ番組に贈られるエミー賞を受賞した。

ll. 25-26……actual education and not marketing

「実際の教育のことでマーケティングではない」。「マーケティング」をここで言うところの「食育 (nutrition education)」ではないとわざわざことわっているのは、第1パラグラフにおいて、ビッグフードの広告などが子どもたちの間に浸透している状況を皮肉の意味で食育としているからである。

l. 59……not A any more than B

= no more A than B 「(主語が) Bでないのと同様Aでない」。Ex. She is not young than I am (young). = She is no more young than I am (young).「私が若くないのと同様、彼女も若くない。」 ／ He cannot swim any more than a hammer. = He can no more swim than a hammer can.「金づちが泳げないのと同様、彼は泳げない。」

l. 60……the Flat Earth Society

「フラット・アース・ソサエティ (平らな地球協会)」とは、地球が球体ではなく、平面であるという古代の考え方を支持する団体。1956年設立。

Checking Your Understanding: True or False

本文の内容に照らして合っているものにはTを、間違えているものにはFを書きなさい。

1. The author is critical of the campaign by the food industry. ☐

2. Jamie Oliver tries to put food education in every school in the U.S. ☐

3. Parents are also responsible for children's food ignorance when they don't teach children how to microwave foods. ☐

4. Teaching geography and algebra is more important than teaching about food. ☐

How to Read a Paragraph

以下の問いに答えなさい。なお、（　）内はヒントとなる段落番号です。

1. "the massive instructional campaign" (ll. 5-6) は、誰が誰に対してどのようなことを教え込むものですか。(Paragraph 1)

   _____

   _____

2. トマトとビーツとカリフラワーの区別がつかないことに対する親たちの反応を本文に即して予測し書きなさい。(Paragraph 3)

   _____

   _____

3. "actual education and not marketing" (ll. 25-26) という挿入句について、"marketing" と "actual education" を対比しながら食育をめぐる状況を説明しなさい。(Paragraph 4)

   _____

   _____

Translating into English

Reading Passages を見ずに、日本語に合うように（　）内の語句を並べ替えて、英文を完成させましょう。冒頭に来る語でも頭文字を小文字にしてあります。

1. 食育はとても重要なのでビッグフードに任せることはできないことは明らかだ。

(to, to, too, important, clear, it's, Big Food, food education, that, leave, is).

_____

2. 子どもたちが食や栄養について学べば学ぶほど、果物や野菜や他の健康的な食品をもっと食べる可能性が高くなる。

(the, about, and, more, learn, food, children, nutrition), (the, to, likely, more, they, eat, are) fruits, vegetables, and other healthful foods.

_____

3. 我々が科学を教えるのをフラット・アース・ソサエティに任すべきではないのと同様、食品業界に食を教えるという重要な仕事を任すべきではない。

(than, more, any, we, we'd, shouldn't, leave, leave, teaching science, the critical task of teaching nutrition, to the food industry) to the Flat Earth Society.

_____

Listening Summary

CD-24

音声を聴き、□内から適切な語を選んで空欄を埋めなさい。

Children in the United States are exposed to a ¹(　　　) manipulative campaign by Big Food, while they don't have much access to ²(　　　) education both at schools and at home. Food education is often the first to be reduced when school budgets are ³(　　　). As a result, children remain ignorant about food and one-third of them are overweight or ⁴(　　　). If they learn how to cook fresh recipes from ⁵(　　　), they will be likely to ⁶(　　　) healthier and various ⁷(　　　). We should call on policymakers to put food education back in every school.

- nutrition
- massive
- appreciate
- obese
- trimmed
- ingredients
- scratch

Unit 12

Tech CEOs Back Call for Basic Income as AI Job Losses Threaten Industry Backlash

IT企業のトップがベーシックインカムを支持する理由

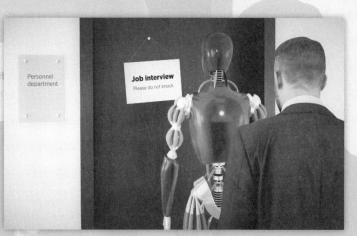

ロボットが人間から職を奪う未来図はつい最近までは SF の世界のなかだけの話だった。しかしながら、人工知能 (AI) の進化のスピードは凄まじく、アメリカでは今後 10 ～ 20 年で半数近くの仕事が自動化 (automation) されると予想する研究者もいる。一方で、労働者の配置転換のうまい手立ても見通しも伝わってこない。このまま行けば、かつて産業革命で機械打ち壊し運動が起きたように、職を脅かされた人々の憎悪が人工知能とテクノロジー企業に向けられ、彼らが「公共の敵ナンバーワン」(public enemy number one) になるのを予想することも難しくはない。テクノロジー企業の最高経営責任者 (CEO) や幹部 (executive) たちが最悪のシナリオを回避するためにした提言とは――。

Matching Words & Phrases

1～10 までの単語の語義を a～j のなかから選んで、線で結びなさい。

1. back [動]
2. backlash
3. wipe out
4. portrayal
5. (be) keen to...
6. drive
7. when it comes to...
8. end up with...
9. convinced
10. displace

a. 推進する、活発にする
b. 描写
c. 確信して
d. …という話になると
e. 解雇する
f. 結果として…になる
g. 一掃する
h. しきりに…したがっている
i. 反発、反動
j. 支援する

Reading Passages

1. It's 2067 and robots have wiped out millions of jobs, AI is rampant, and unemployment is on the rise. Technology companies and CEOs have become public enemy number one.

2. This portrayal of the future is one tech executives are keen to avoid and has driven a growing chorus to support the idea of a universal basic income (UBI). "There is going to be backlash when it comes to jobs," Sayantan Ghosal, an economics professor at the University of Glasgow who has written about UBI, told CNBC by phone.

3. Over the past few months, major technology executives have come out in support of a UBI. In an interview with CNBC in November, Tesla Chief Executive Elon Musk backed the idea. "There is a pretty good chance we end up with a universal basic income, or something like that, due to automation," Musk said.

4. Experts say that the tech industry is growing more aware of its role in driving future automation and displacement, and companies don't want to be at the heart of any backlash from workers. "That is a factor. The concern that suddenly public enemy number one will be robots and they (tech firms) will be in the firing line," Guy Standing, professorial research associate at the School of Oriental and African Studies, told CNBC by phone.

5. How a basic income project might work in the future is unclear and the technology industry is still not sure. One idea is for governments to pay everyone a monthly sum. Experts say it will not disincentivize workers because it will provide a bare minimum of living. Instead, workers will still want to get a higher standard of living by working.

6. But any policy will be tough to fund.

7. One way for governments to pay for a UBI is through

a sovereign wealth fund, where they take a small two to three percent equity stake in all the publicly listed companies in the country and earn money in that way.

⑧ Another idea that CEOs are slowly turning towards, is the taxing of "super profits," according to Standing. The academic told CNBC that a major technology CEO he spoke to said that he was convinced the industry would need to start making "concessions" in the form of taxing more profits.

⑨ Microsoft founder Bill Gates recently floated the idea of a "robot tax" as a way for governments to get more money in the future. "If a human worker does $50,000 of work in a factory, that income is taxed," Gates said in a recent interview with Quartz. "If a robot comes in to do the same thing, you'd think we'd tax the robot at a similar level."

⑩ Academics like Standing and Ghosal say that like previous technological revolutions, workers are likely to be displaced, then retrain and get back into work. UBI would still let people work, but would give them some support as they find new skills.

The Keys to Reading Passages

l. 7 …… universal basic income
「ベーシックインカム」、もしくは「最低所得保障」とも言われる。政府がすべての国民に対して必要最低限の生活を送るのに必要な額を無条件で支給する政策・制度。

l. 10 …… CNBC
正式名称は Consumer News and Business Channel。アメリカのニュース専門局。この記事は CNBC によるものである。

l. 14 …… Tesla
「テスラ社」とは、主に電気自動車を開発・販売しているアメリカの自動車メーカー。自動運転車の開発にも力を入れている。

l. 36 …… sovereign wealth fund
「政府系ファンド」、もしくはそのまま「ソブリン・ウェルス・ファンド」とも言われる。政府が出資する政府系投資機関が運用するファンドで、国の余剰資金（通常は貿易黒字による外貨準備高や天然資源による収入など）を原資とし、将来の世代のための資金の蓄えなどを目的として運用される。

l. 40 …… super profit
新技術の開発や新商品の開発などで、想定される利潤（平均利潤）以上に多く得られた利潤のこと。テクノロジー企業は AI 技術の活用によって有利な生産条件を独占的に維持し、莫大な「超過利潤」を継続的に得ることが見込まれる。

Checking Your Understanding: True or False

📝 本文の内容に照らして合っているものにはTを、間違えているものにはFを書きなさい。

1. Elon Musk thought that it was highly probable that a UBI would be introduced due to automation. ☐

2. It is certain that a basic income project will work out well. ☐

3. It is difficult for governments to raise funds for a UBI. ☐

4. UBI will discourage people. ☐

How to Read a Paragraph

📝 以下の問いに答えなさい。なお、（ ）内はヒントとなる段落番号です。

1. テクノロジー企業の幹部たちはなぜベーシックインカムの導入に賛成しているのですか。 (Paragraphs 1, 2 & 4)

   _____
   _____

2. Paragraph 7 では、政府系ファンドを通して、ベーシックインカムの資金をどのようにまかなう案が出されていますか。

   _____
   _____

3. ビル・ゲイツ氏の提唱するロボット税とはどのようなものですか。(Paragraph 9)

   _____
   _____

Translating into English

Reading Passages を見ずに、日本語に合うように（　）内の語句を並び替えて、英文を完成させましょう。冒頭に来る語でも頭文字を小文字にしてあります。

1. 職という話になれば反動があるだろう。
   There (to, to, when, going, be, comes, is, it, jobs, backlash).

   _____

2. どんな政策も資金をまかなうのが大変である。
   (to, any, be, will, tough, fund, policy).

   _____

3. 彼は、業界が超過した利益に課税する形で譲歩をし始める必要があるだろうと確信していた。
   (the, to, would, making, convinced, need, was, start, concessions, he, industry) in the form of taxing more profits.

   _____

Listening Summary

CD-26

音声を聴き、□内から適切な語を選んで空欄を埋めなさい。

Recently, major technology ¹(　　　) have declared that they ²(　　　) the idea of a UBI. According to experts, the technology industry has become more conscious of its role in ³(　　　) future automation and displacement. Tech executives are ⁴(　　　) to avoid any ⁵(　　　) from workers when AI ⁶(　　　) out most of jobs and workers are likely to be ⁷(　　　) in the future. However, nobody knows whether a UBI will be effective.

● wipes ● back ● driving ● backlash ● displaced ● keen ● executives

Unit 13

Cramer Pinpoints the 'Best Secular Trend' in the Market: Subscription Services

「モノ所有」から「利用」へ——サブスクリプション経済のビジネスモデル

モノが売れなくなったことの説明の一つがシェアリング経済の普及である。もう一つには、あらゆるビジネスモデルがモノの所有から「利用」へ切り替わりつつある現象があげられる。それがサブスクリプション経済 (subscription economy) である。サブスクリプションとはいわゆる「定額制使い放題」のサービスのことで、すでに音楽や映像配信サービスで私たちにもなじみのものとなっている。いま、音楽や映像だけに限らず、思いもよらない産業も含め、あらゆる産業が一斉にこのビジネスモデルへ舵を切り始めた。本文では投資家ジム・クレイマー氏 (Jim Cramer) がこのトレンドを語る。

Matching Words & Phrases

1〜10までの単語の語義をa〜jのなかから選んで、線で結びなさい。

1. secular — a. 意味をなす
2. make sense — b. 乗っ取る
3. reflect — c. 意見を述べる
4. carve — d. 小売業者
5. revenue — e. 長期的な（▶「世俗的な」という意味もある）
6. deal — f. 収益
7. loyal — g. 開拓する、切り開く
8. retailer — h. 結論
9. bottom line — i. 忠実な
10. take over — j. お得なもの、お買い得品

Reading Passages

[1] "The best secular trend out there right now? ... I think it's the rise of the subscription economy, the legion of companies that make their money by selling some kind of subscription service, often in industries where we never even realized subscriptions could make any sense," CNBC's Jim Cramer said Friday.

[2] After speaking with the founder, Chairman and CEO of Zuora, a newly public software company that sees itself as a "pure play" on the subscription economy, Cramer's perspective on the trend completely changed.

[3] "There's no reason you should have to buy anything," Tien Tzuo, the Zuora chief, told Cramer in a Thursday interview. "We used to have Netflix, we used to have Spotify, but now, we're paying for exercise bikes as a subscription, we're paying for travel as a subscription, ... companies are [even] paying for things like tractor[s] as a subscription."

[4] Tzuo, who wrote a book on the "subscription-based economy," suggested to Cramer that this model isn't going away. "The point here is that, like it or not, the subscription economy is the future and the companies that understand that are making a fortune", Cramer reflected.

[5] Take the aforementioned Netflix and Spotify, two Cramer-fave companies that were born out of the demand for easier access to movies and music. "They're subscription services as a gateway drug," Cramer said. "By paying a low monthly fee, you get access to a whole world of entertainment."

[6] With 125 million subscribers, a growing library of original content and global reach, Netflix has become a monolith in the subscription economy. Shares of the streaming giant have more than doubled in 2018.

[7] Spotify, the Netflix of music, has 71 million premium subscribers — those who pay up to use its free service

without advertisements — and has seen 46 percent premium subscriber growth in the last year.

⑧ Apple may not seem like a subscription-service play, but the iPhone maker is carving a space for itself in the subscription economy with its budding razor-razorblade model, Cramer said. "The phones are the razors and the various subscription services that you pay for automatically are the blades," he said.

⑨ Apple's revenue for its subscription services like Apple Music and iCloud storage grew by 31 percent in the last quarter, blowing past expectations to a $9.2 billion total. "If Apple's subscription biz were its own company, it would already be large enough to be about a Fortune 80 company," Cramer said.

⑩ Cramer also touted Amazon Prime as one of the most successful renditions of the subscription economy. The service offers members free shipping, video streaming and music as well as countless deals. "The key here is that Prime creates legions of loyal customers who have a huge incentive to shop at Amazon first and only go to another retailer if they can't find what they need," he said.

⑪ "The bottom line? The subscription economy keeps taking over industry after industry after industry after industry because it's so darned lucrative and consumers love it," Cramer said.

The Keys to Reading Passages

l. 6 …… Jim Cramer
「ジム・クレイマー」は CNBC で投資情報番組 "Mad Money" を持つ投資家である。本文は、"Mad Money" でクレイマー氏が語ったことを元に書かれた記事である。

l. 8 …… Zuora
「ズオラ」はサブスクリプションビジネスを提供する企業をクラウド（インターネットを経由して提供されるサービス）で支援する企業である。顧客が従来のプロダクト販売モデル（「モノ所有」）からサブスクリプションモデル（「利用」）に切り替えるために最適化されたアプリケーションを開発・販売・提供している。

l. 9 …… pure play
1 種類の製品・サービスだけを扱う企業、もしくは店舗を持たずインターネット上だけで商売する会社。ズオラ社は両方に当てはまるが、この部分ではサブスクリプション経済に特化したサービスを扱う会社であることを指している。

l. 13 …… Netflix
映像ストリーミング配信サービス会社。（ストリーミングとは、インターネットで映像や音声などを視聴する際、データを受信しながら同時に再生する方式。）月額を払うとコンテンツが見放題である。

l. 14 …… Spotify
音楽ストリーミング配信サービス会社。サービスは無料の Spotify Free と月額制の Spotify Premium の 2 種類があり、いずれもコンテンツが聴き放題である。この 2 種類がどのように違うかは本文から読み取ってみよう。

l. 27 …… gateway drug
そのまま「ゲートウェイドラッグ」とも言われ、元々の意味はより強い麻薬の常用形成への入り口となるアルコールやマリファナなどのことを指すが、ここではサブスクリプションサービスの文脈で比喩的に用いられていることに注意。

l. 40-41 …… razor-razorblade model
「カミソリとカミソリの刃モデル」。カミソリ本体を購入すれば、消耗品であるカミソリの刃を定期的に購入しなければならないので、カミソリ本体を売る意味はその利益を得る以上のねらいがある。これをサブスクリプションビジネスに当てはめて考えてみよう。

l. 48-49 …… a Fortune 80 company
「フォーチュン誌の発表するリストのトップ 80 の企業」。『フォーチュン』誌は世界最大の英文ビジネス雑誌で、毎年フォーチュン・リストと呼ばれるランキングを発表しており、「フォーチュン 100」では、全米上位 100 社をランキングしている。

l. 50 …… Amazon Prime
アマゾンに月額もしくは年額を払いプライム会員になると受けられるサービス全般を指す。

Checking Your Understanding: True or False

本文の内容に照らして合っているものには T を、間違えているものには F を書きなさい。

1. The subscription economy has been spreading in industries which seemed to have nothing to do with subscriptions.

2. A subscription service for travel is not available now.

3. Spotify premium subscribers can enjoy music without advertisements.

4. Apple's subscription service company is one of Fortune 80 companies.

How to Read a Paragraph

以下の問いに答えなさい。なお、( ) 内はヒントとなる段落番号です。

1. カミソリとカミソリの刃モデルとはどのようなものか、具体的にアップル社に当てはめて説明しなさい。(Paragraph 8)

2. アマゾンはアマゾンプライムでサブスクリプションサービスを提供することによって、どのような利点がありますか。(Paragraph 10)

3. Paragraph 11 において、なぜクレイマー氏は "after industry" を 3 回も繰り返したのですか。

Translating into English

Reading Passages を見ずに、日本語に合うように（　）内の語句を並び替えて、英文を完成させましょう。冒頭に来る語でも頭文字を小文字にしてあります。

1. 安い月額料金を支払うことによって、エンターテイメントの世界にまるごとアクセスできる。
   (a, by, low, monthly, paying, fee), (a, to, of, whole, get, world, access, entertainment, you).

2. そのストリーミング最大手企業のシェアは 2018 年には 2 倍以上になった。
   (the, of, than, more, doubled, have, streaming, shares, giant) in 2018.

3. Apple Music や iCloud ストレージのようなアップル社のサブスクリプションサービスの収益は直前の四半期で 31% 伸びた。
   Apple's revenue (by, for, and, its, like, grew, Apple Music, iCloud storage, subscription services, 31 percent) in the last quarter.

Listening Summary

音声を聴き、□内から適切な語を選んで空欄を埋めなさい。

CD-28

Tien Tzuo, the chief of Zuora, a newly established ¹(　　　) software company, completely changed Jim Cramer's ²(　　　) on the ³(　　　) economy. Tzuo told Cramer that we could use anything as a subscription and didn't have to buy anything. Cramer ⁴(　　　) that the companies that understood this trend would make a ⁵(　　　) and the ⁶(　　　) line was that the subscription economy continued to ⁷(　　　) over various industries.

- take
- public
- bottom
- subscription
- reflected
- perspective
- fortune

Unit 14

World Bank Warns Over South Asian Climate 'Hotspots' as Crops and Livelihoods Hit

気候変動と温室効果ガスに対する2つのシナリオ

近頃、命の危険を感じるような暑さが続く日本の夏であるが、この猛暑は日本だけに限らず世界的な現象である。そして、暑さだけにとどまらず、様々な面で今まで経験したことのないような異常気象 (extreme weather) が続いていると感じる人も多いだろう。気候変動 (climate change) が世界中で続いているなか、世界銀行 (the World Bank) は、この気候変動による2050年の姿を予測した研究を発表した。それによると、最も影響を受けるのがインドをはじめとした南アジアの地域であり、現在8億人以上がそれらの地域に住んでいると言う。気候変動の原因となる地球温暖化を食い止め、そのような未来を変えるには何ができるのだろうか。

Matching Words & Phrases

1〜10までの単語の語義をa〜jのなかから選んで、線で結びなさい。

1. have a glimpse of...　　a. 熟する
2. pose　　　　　　　　　b. 以前の
3. livelihood　　　　　　　c. 仮定する、想定する
4. ripen　　　　　　　　　d. 危険な
5. inhabitant　　　　　　　e. （困難な状況などを）引き起こす、（脅威などを）もたらす
6. shift　　　　　　　　　f. （状況などが）変わる
7. reliant (on)　　　　　　g. ちらりと見る、かいま見る
8. assume　　　　　　　　h. （特定地域・家などの）住人
9. previous　　　　　　　i. 依存した、当てにした
10. precarious　　　　　　j. 暮らし、生計

Reading Passages

[1] Sweltering under the record temperatures of a blistering hot spring, Pakistan's farmers have this year had a vivid glimpse of the dangers a changing climate may pose to their livelihoods. The scorching weather of 2018 follows a trend of increasingly short, warm and early spring seasons which have left Pakistan's farmers struggling to deal with new weather patterns. The heat has dried out farmland and hit profits by causing fruit and vegetables to ripen earlier, but smaller.

[2] New research from the World Bank attempting to quantify how climate change will affect South Asia over the coming decades has now warned weather changes risk badly denting the living standards of hundreds of millions in the region. More than 800 million of South Asia's inhabitants live in predicted climate change "hotspots" where living standards will fall significantly without action to limit greenhouse gases.

[3] As temperatures rise and rainfall patterns shift, difficulties with farming, irrigation, disease and labour are predicted by 2050 to badly hit people's quality of living in parts of India, Pakistan and Bangladesh. The impact due to changing average weather patterns will be worst inland and most severe in already poor areas reliant on farming and short of water, according to climate and economic models. India will have most of the hotspots.

[4] Researchers at the bank ran two different scenarios for the effects of climate change, based on whether action is taken to limit greenhouse gases. Under a "carbon intensive" scenario which assumes no action on climate change, more than 800 million people now live in areas where annual household consumption spending will fall by at least 4 per cent by the middle of the century. The bank judged moderate hotspots as areas where projected consumption spending declines by 4-8 percent and severe

ones are where the drop exceeds 8 percent.

5 "Changes in the Earth's climate will have major effects on the people of South Asia, which is already one of the most affected regions of the world," said Annette Dixon, the bank's South Asia vice president.

6 The bank said most previous predictions had looked at the damage rising sea levels and extreme weather could wreak. That research highlighted precarious coastal areas vulnerable to storms and flooding. Looking at the long-term results of gradually rising average temperatures had instead highlighted the risk to interior areas, the bank said. "Hotspots are identified where people could be most severely affected by changes in average temperature and precipitation. Many of these are in locations that hitherto have not been seen as particularly vulnerable to climate."

7 Under the worst case "carbon intensive" scenario, living standards will fall by 6.7 percent for Bangladesh, 2.8 percent for India, 2.9 percent for Pakistan, and 7.0 percent for Sri Lanka, by 2050, the bank said.

8 Under the second scenario, where action is taken to tackle greenhouse gases, living standards still fall, but for fewer people. Under that scenario, the predicted hotspots currently support around 280 million people.

The Keys to Reading Passages

l. 16⋯⋯ hotspot

「ホットスポット、危険な場所（状況）」。英英辞典を引くと、「周囲に比べて比較的高温な小さなエリア」というのが元々の意味で出てくるが、転じて比喩的に「危険な場所や状況」、「活気がある人気スポット」などの意味で使われると書いてある。そのまま「ホットスポット」と日本語で使われることも多いが、文脈に応じて指している状況を理解する必要がある。

l. 17⋯⋯ greenhouse gas

「温室効果ガス」とは、地球温暖化を引き起こすガスのことで、地球上の大気に含まれる主に二酸化炭素やメタンなどの気体の総称。「それらの気体は、赤外線を吸収し、また、再放射する性質を有する。そのため、太陽に温められた地球表面から放射される赤外線の多くが、熱として大気に蓄積され地球に戻ってくる。その戻ってきた赤外線が、地球の表面付近の大気を温め、温室効果、すなわち、地球温暖化をもたらす」（『日本大百科全書』より）。ここで話題になっている気候変動は「温室効果ガス」が引き金になっていると考えられている。また、人為的な産業活動に伴って排出される温室効果ガス（の排出量の増加）が地球温暖化の原因と見なされているため、いかに措置を講じるかが地球の未来、とりわけホットスポットになると予測されている南アジアの未来を決めることになる。

l. 29-30⋯⋯ "carbon intensive" scenario

「『（主たる温室効果ガスの気体である）二酸化炭素排出量の多い』シナリオ」、すなわち温室効果ガスに対して規制措置を講じないというシナリオがここでなぜ想定されているかというと、トランプ大統領をはじめ地球温暖化及び人為的に排出される温室効果ガスが温暖化を引き起こすことに対する懐疑派が根強くいるからである。長い歴史のなかで氷河期や温暖期が繰り返されてきたし、地球温暖化はあったとしても自然的要因であるとし、温室効果ガス排出量規制にも消極的なのが懐疑派である。しかしながら、世界的に起こっている近頃の異常気象（とりわけ、猛暑）を目の当たりにして、懐疑派はどのように思っているのだろうか。

Checking Your Understanding: True or False

📝 本文の内容に照らして合っているものにはTを、間違えているものにはFを書きなさい。

1. Climate change involves rises in temperature and shifts in rainfall patterns. ☐

2. Coastal areas will have more hotspots than inland ones. ☐

3. South Asia has been already affected by climate change. ☐

4. Living standards of inhabitants living in predicted hotspots will stay the same under the second scenario. ☐

How to Read a Paragraph

📝 以下の問いに答えなさい。なお、( ) 内はヒントとなる段落番号です。

1. "Two different scenarios" (l. 27) とは、どのようなことに基づいて、どのようなものに対して、作られたシナリオですか。(**Paragraph 4**)

   _____

   _____

2. 以前の研究ではどのような地域が危険とされており、それに対して世界銀行の研究ではどのような地域が危険とされていますか。(**Paragraph 6**)

   _____

   _____

3. "The second scenario" (l. 56) について、どのような仮定に基づいたシナリオで、どのくらいの人々に影響があるとしていますか。(**Paragraph 8**)

   _____

   _____

Translating into English

Reading Passages を見ずに、日本語に合うように（　）内の語句を並び替えて、英文を完成させましょう。冒頭に来る語でも頭文字を小文字にしてあります。

1. パキスタンの農家たちは、変動する気候が彼らの暮らしにもたらす危険をはっきりとかいま見てきた。

(a, the, of, vivid, have, glimpse, had, dangers, Pakistan's farmers) (a, their, may, pose, changing, to, climate, livelihoods).

_____

2. 平均的な気候パターンの変動に起因する影響は、すでに農業に依存し水不足の貧しいエリアでは最も深刻なものとなるだろう。

The impact due to changing average weather patterns will be (on, of, in, and, reliant, severe, already, short, poor, most, farming, areas, water).

_____

3. 世界銀行は中程度のホットスポットを予測される消費支出が4～8％下落する地域と判断した。

The bank judged moderate hotspots as (by, where, projected, spending, declines, consumption, 4-8 percent, areas).

_____

Listening Summary

CD-30

音声を聴き、☐内から適切な語を選んで空欄を埋めなさい。

A new World Bank research finds that more than 800 million of South Asian ¹(　　　) are at risk of seeing their living ²(　　　) fall significantly by 2050 due to changing average weather patterns, which creates ³(　　　) across South Asia. More than 800 million South Asians live in ⁴(　　　) climate change hotspots. The Bank shows two future climate ⁵(　　　) based on whether action is taken to ⁶(　　　) greenhouse gases. If we take action to tackle ⁷(　　　) gases, we can reduce the damage.

- greenhouse
- predicted
- hotspots
- inhabitants
- limit
- standard
- scenarios

Unit 15

First-of-its-kind Clinical Trial Will Use Reprogrammed Adult Stem Cells to Treat Parkinson's

世界初パーキンソン病への iPS 細胞治験開始

©読売新聞社

幹細胞 (stem cell) とは、分裂して自分と同じ細胞を生む能力 (自己複製能) と分化して専門の機能を果たす細胞 (specialized cell) になる能力 (分化能) を合わせ持つ細胞のことであり、タイトルの成体幹細胞 (adult stem cell) は体内の幹細胞を意味する。すなわち、幹細胞は身体の部位を再生修復する能力を持つ。その中で、あらゆる組織や臓器の細胞に分化する能力 (多能性、pluripotent) を持つのが多能性幹細胞であり、その代表的なものが iPS 細胞である。iPS 細胞は、再生医療への応用はもちろん、病気の原因の解明、新薬の開発を飛躍的に進めることが期待されている。2018 年、治療法が確立されていないパーキンソン病の治験 (clinical trial) が始まった。

Matching Words & Phrases

1〜10 までの単語の語義を a〜j のなかから選んで、線で結びなさい。

1. (be) derived from... 　　a. 注入する
2. theoretically 　　b. …に由来する
3. inject 　　c. 条件付きの
4. involuntary 　　d. 免疫の
5. strategy 　　e. 承認する
6. last [動] 　　f. (細胞の) 組織
7. immune 　　g. 続く
8. approve 　　h. 無意識な、不随意の
9. tissue 　　i. 理論上は
10. conditional 　　j. 計画、戦略

Reading Passages

1 Researchers in Japan today announced the launch of a clinical trial to treat Parkinson's disease with neurological material derived from induced pluripotent stem (iPS) cells, mature cells chemically manipulated to return to an early stage of development from which they can theoretically differentiate into any of the body's specialized cells.

2 The study team will inject dopaminergic progenitors, a cell type that develops into neurons that produce dopamine, directly into a region of the brain known to play a key role in the neural degeneration associated with Parkinson's disease. The effort is being led by Jun Takahashi, a neurosurgeon at Kyoto University's Center for iPS Cell Research and Application (CiRA), in cooperation with Kyoto University Hospital.

3 Parkinson's disease results from the death of specialized cells in the brain that produce the neurotransmitter dopamine. A lack of dopamine leads to a decline in motor skills, resulting in difficulty walking and involuntary trembling. As the disease progresses it can lead to dementia. The trial strategy is to derive dopaminergic progenitors from iPS cells and inject them into the putamen, a round structure located at the base of the forebrain. Surgeons will drill two small holes through a patient's skull and use a specialized device to inject roughly 5 million cells.

4 Studies in animals have shown that the progenitors differentiate into dopaminergic neurons inside the body and engraft into the brain. Takahashi's group reported last year that monkey models of Parkinson's disease showed significant improvement lasting 2 years after getting injections of neurons prepared from human iPS cells.

5 Rather than make patient-specific iPS cells, CiRA has adopted the strategy of deriving stocks of iPS cells

from healthy donors with specific cell types that are less likely to cause immune rejection. "Using stocks of cells, we can proceed much more quickly and cost-effectively," CiRA Director Shinya Yamanaka, who won a share of the Nobel Prize in Physiology or Medicine in 2012 for discovering how to create iPS cells, told *Science* in 2017. As an added precaution, the patients will receive a common immunosuppressant in tandem with the progenitors.

6 Patient recruitment started today at 5 p.m. local time, when Kyoto University Hospital posted the patient recruitment notice on its website. The team plans to recruit seven patients and follow them for 2 years postinjection.

7 This is the third human trial using iPS cells approved in Japan. The first, using retinal cells derived from iPS cells to replace eye tissue damaged by age-related macular degeneration (AMD), was launched in 2014 and is being led by Masayo Takahashi—Jun Takahashi's wife—of the RIKEN Center for Developmental Biology in Kobe. The AMD treatment was initially reported to be safe, though there has been one reported adverse event. Earlier this year, a team at Osaka University in Japan won conditional approval for an iPS cell-based study for ischemic heart disease.

The Keys to Reading Passages・・・・・・・・・・・・・・・

l. 3-4 …… induced pluripotent stem (iPS) cell

「iPS 細胞」、正式名称は「人工多能性幹細胞」。iPS 細胞とは、「人間の皮膚などの体細胞に、ごく少数の因子を導入し、培養することによって、様々な組織や臓器の細胞に分化する能力と、ほぼ無限に増殖する能力を持つ多能性幹細胞に変化」した細胞。「体細胞が多能性幹細胞に変わることを、専門用語でリプログラミング」と言う。なお、「名付け親は、世界で初めて iPS 細胞の作製に成功した」京都大学の山中伸弥教授である。また、同じ幹細胞として期待される ES 細胞に比べて画期的な点は、「ES 細胞は受精後 6、7 日目の胚盤胞から細胞を取り出し、それを培養することによって作製され」る、「一方、iPS 細胞は皮膚や血液など、採取しやすい体細胞を使って作ることができ」る点と、「ES 細胞と違って、iPS 細胞は患者さん自身の細胞から作製することができ、分化した組織や臓器の細胞を移植した場合、拒絶反応が起こりにくいと考えられ」ている点である（京都大学 iPS 細胞研究所 HP より）。

l. 4 …… mature cell

「成熟（した）細胞」⇒ differentiate into の項目を参照。

l. 6 …… differentiate into

幹細胞が分化（誘導）すると、特定の機能を持つ細胞（specialized cell）に変化する。分化誘導を終えた細胞 [最終分化細胞]（specialized cell、mature cell とも本文では表現されている）は他の細胞に変化しない。分化が行われて最終分化細胞になる一歩手前の細胞を「前駆細胞」（progenitor cell）と呼ぶ。すなわち、幹細胞は前駆細胞を経て最終分化細胞へと分化する。

l. 8 …… dopaminergic progenitor

「ドーパミン神経前駆細胞」とは、「ドーパミン神経細胞に分化する手前の細胞」である。「前駆細胞」については、differentiate into の項を参照。「パーキンソン病モデル動物を用いた研究から、ドーパミン神経前駆細胞を移植することによって脳内に成熟ドーパミン神経細胞を効率的に生着させられることが明らかになって」いる（京都大学 iPS 細胞研究所 HP より）。

l. 55 …… the RIKEN Center for Developmental Biology

「理化学研究所多細胞システム形成研究センター」

Checking Your Understanding: True or False

本文の内容に照らして合っているものにはTを、間違えているものにはFを書きなさい。

1. The putamen is a region of the brain known to play a key role in the neural degeneration associated with Parkinson's disease. ☐

2. Takahashi's team will derive dopaminergic progenitors from dopamine. ☐

3. Takahashi's group reported injections of neurons derived from human iPS cells was effective in monkey models of Parkinson's diseases. ☐

4. The first human clinical trial using iPS cells approved in Japan was carried out successfully. ☐

How to Read a Paragraph

以下の問いに答えなさい。なお、（　）内はヒントとなる段落番号です。

1. iPS細胞のPはpluripotent（多能性、万能）の略であるが、理論的にどのようなことが可能であるがゆえに万能と言われるのか説明しなさい。(Paragraph 1)

   _____
   _____

2. パーキンソン病の原因を説明しなさい。(Paragraph 3)

   _____
   _____

3. 治験において、個体別のiPS細胞を作らずにストックのiPS細胞を使う利点をすべて挙げなさい。(Paragraph 5)

   _____
   _____

Translating into English

Reading Passages を見ずに、日本語に合うように（　）内の語句を並び替えて、英文を完成させましょう。冒頭に来る語でも頭文字を小文字にしてあります。

1. 日本において研究者たちは、iPS 細胞由来の神経物質を使った、パーキンソン病を治療するための治験の始動を発表した。

    Researchers in Japan (a, the, to, of, clinical, announced, launch, treat, trial, Parkinson's disease) with (from, derived, neurological material, iPS cells).

    _____

2. 病気が進行するにつれて、認知症に至る可能性もある。

    (the, to, as, can, lead, progresses, dementia, disease, it).

    _____

3. これが日本で承認された iPS 細胞を用いた人間の治験の 3 例目となる。

    (the, this, third, is, using, approved, trial, iPS cells, human) in Japan.

    _____

Listening Summary

CD-32

音声を聴き、□内から適切な語を選んで空欄を埋めなさい。

A Kyoto University research team announced it would ¹(　　　) a clinical trial using iPS cells to treat Parkinson's disease. iPS cells can ²(　　　) into any type of body ³(　　　). Parkinson's disease results from neural degeneration, reduces dopamine in the brain and results in difficulty walking and ⁴(　　　) trembling. The ⁵(　　　) is to inject nerve cells derived from iPS cells into the brain and observe patients for two years after the injection. The nerve cells are created using iPS cells from ⁶(　　　) who have specific cell types that make them less prone to ⁷(　　　) rejection.

- involuntary
- immune
- donors
- launch
- tissue
- differentiate
- strategy

JPCA 日本出版著作権協会
http://www.jpca.jp.net/

本書は日本出版著作権協会（JPCA）が委託管理する著作物です。
複写（コピー）・複製、その他著作物の利用については、事前に JPCA（電話 03-3812-9424, e-mail:info@e-jpca.com）の許諾を得て下さい。なお、無断でコピー・スキャン・デジタル化等の複製をすることは著作権法上の例外を除き、著作権法違反となります。

---

15 Topics for Tomorrow's World
世界の未来を占う最重要トピック 15

2019 年 4 月　5 日　初版第 1 刷発行
2020 年 3 月 10 日　初版第 2 刷発行

編著者　宮本　文

発行者　森　信久
発行所　株式会社　松 柏 社
　　　　〒102-0072　東京都千代田区飯田橋 1-6-1
　　　　TEL 03 (3230) 4813（代表）
　　　　FAX 03 (3230) 4857
　　　　http://www.shohakusha.com
　　　　e-mail: info@shohakusha.com

装　　丁　　小島トシノブ（NONdesign）
本文レイアウト　株式会社クリエーターズユニオン（一柳　茂）
印刷・製本　　日経印刷株式会社

略号＝ 741
ISBN978-4-88198-741-4
Copyright © 2019 by Aya Miyamoto

本書を無断で複写・複製することを禁じます。